WORLDS TOGETHER, WORLDS APART

A Companion Reader

WORLDS TOGETHER, WORLDS APART

VOLUME 1

A Companion Reader

EDITED BY

KENNETH L. POMERANZ
JAMES B. GIVEN
LAURA J. MITCHELL

W · W · NORTON & COMPANY
NEW YORK · LONDON

W. W. Norton & Company has been independent since its founding in 1923, when William Warder Norton and Mary D. Herter Norton first published lectures delivered at the People's Institute, the adult education division of New York City's Cooper Union. The firm soon expanded its program beyond the Institute, publishing books by celebrated academics from America and abroad. By midcentury, the two major pillars of Norton's publishing program—trade books and college texts—were firmly established. In the 1950s, the Norton family transferred control of the company to its employees, and today—with a staff of four hundred and a comparable number of trade, college, and professional titles published each year—W. W. Norton & Company stands as the largest and oldest publishing house owned wholly by its employees.

Book design and composition by Westchester Book Group
Production manager: Ben Reynolds

Library of Congress Cataloging-in-Publication Data

Worlds together, worlds apart : a companion reader / edited by Kenneth L. Pomeranz, James B. Given, Laura J. Mitchell.
    p. cm.
    Companion to: Worlds together, worlds apart : a history of the world from the beginnings of humankind to the present / Robert Tignor . . . [et al.].
    Includes bibliographical references and index.
    ISBN 978-0-393-91160-2 (v. 1)—ISBN 978-0-393-91161-9 (v. 2)
1. World history—Sources. I. Pomeranz, Kenneth. II. Given, James Buchanan. III. Mitchell, Laura Jane, 1963– IV. Tignor, Robert L.
    D21.W939 2011
    909—dc22

2010038550

W. W. Norton & Company, Inc., 500 Fifth Avenue, New York, NY 10110
  wwnorton.com

W. W. Norton & Company Ltd., Castle House, 75/76 Wells Street, London W1T 3QT

1 2 3 4 5 6 7 8 9 0

About the Editors

KENNETH L. POMERANZ (Ph.D. Yale University) is Chancellor's Professor of History at the University of California, Irvine. His publications include *The Great Divergence: China, Europe, and the Making of the Modern World Economy*; *The Making of a Hinterland: State, Society and Economy in Inland North China, 1853–1937*; and numerous other works. He is a Fellow of the American Academy of Arts and Sciences.

JAMES B. GIVEN (Ph.D. Stanford University) is professor of medieval history at the University of California, Irvine. His principal interests are the social and religious history of Europe in the thirteenth and fourteenth centuries. His works include *Society and Homicide in Thirteenth-Century England*, *State and Society in Medieval Europe: Gwynedd and Languedoc under Outside Rule*, and *Inquisition and Medieval Society: Power, Discipline, and Resistance in Languedoc*.

LAURA J. MITCHELL (Ph.D. University of California, Los Angeles) is associate professor of African history at UC Irvine. She has served on the World History Association Executive Council and is co-chair of the AP World History Curriculum Assessment and Development Committee. Her book *Belongings: Property, Family, and Identity in Colonial South Africa* (Columbia University Press, 2009) is available online at www.gutenberg-e.org/mitchell.

To our students, graduate and undergraduate,
in world history

CONTENTS

*Visual Source

CHAPTER 3 | NOMADS, TERRITORIAL STATES, AND MICROSOCIETIES, 2000–1200 BCE

CASEBOOK | WOMEN AND POLITICAL POWER IN THE ANCIENT WORLD

CHAPTER 4 | FIRST EMPIRES AND COMMON CULTURES IN AFRO-EURASIA, 1200–350 BCE

CHAPTER 5 | WORLDS TURNED INSIDE OUT, 1000–350 BCE

CHAPTER 6 | SHRINKING THE AFRO-EURASIAN WORLD, 350 BCE–300 CE

CHAPTER 7 | HAN DYNASTY CHINA AND IMPERIAL ROME, 300 BCE–300 CE

CHAPTER 8 | THE RISE OF UNIVERSAL RELIGIONS, 300–600 CE

CHAPTER 9 | NEW EMPIRES AND COMMON CULTURES, 600–1000 CE

CHAPTER 10 | BECOMING "THE WORLD," 1000–1300 CE

CASEBOOK | MOBILIZING FOR WAR IN THE AGE OF THE MONGOLS

CHAPTER 11 | CRISES AND RECOVERY IN AFRO-EURASIA, 1300S–1500S

Preface

An all-news radio station used to promise, "You give us 22 minutes, we give you the world." This book, however, will not "give" you world history. Nearly one hundred and fifty documents cannot be comprehensive, or even representative. Some documents, of course, reveal a great deal about a particularly important moment. A classic example is Bishop Eusebius of Caesarea's account of the Roman emperor Constantine's early fourth-century conversion to Christianity. But most great events—not to mention long-term trends and transformations—cannot be captured in a single text.

This book, however, can help students learn how to read primary sources and enrich their studies. For years, the history faculty at the University of California–Irvine have made the teaching of primary sources a centerpiece of our world history survey course. Many of us have also used *Worlds Together, Worlds Apart* since its first publication because it reinforces many of our course objectives. This document collection reflects our best effort to provide you with a diverse range of primary sources that we know to work well in class, and ones that will complement the main themes and existing primary sources in *Worlds Together, Worlds Apart*.

A number of factors influenced our document selection process. We have chosen items we know work well in the classroom, sometimes passing over more famous texts. For example, instead of including Newton's laws of gravity and universal motion (the foundation of modern physics), we have chosen a map that shows how the sources from which he gathered information for his work corresponded to early modern trade routes. Not only is the map easier to discuss outside the context of a physics class; it provides insights about how one set of specifically global *historical* transformations, in this case the expansion of information networks as maritime trade boomed, influenced science. This document also reflects our attention to a range of visual sources. We have included paintings, representations of objects, photographs, maps, and charts for the obvious reason that not all historical evidence is textual, but more importantly because in our experience, studying a wide range of sources and types of material is the best way to foster new ways of thinking about historical problems.

We selected documents that help the reader see "how," in Charles Tilly's phrase, "the little people lived the big changes." We have tried to cover major events, and provide documents for each period from various parts of the world, but we have been more concerned to present documents that start and sustain conversations about important *themes* which turn up, with variations, in many times and places. For example, Xu Jie's commentary (see Chapter 14) describes how relations between landlords and tenants changed in sixteenth-century China as the economy commercialized, the rich moved to towns, free tenants resisted being treated like servants, and the renting of land became a set of cash transactions between near-strangers. These trends did not occur together only in sixteenth-century Songjiang, nor were the results the same wherever and whenever they occurred. This document cannot stand for the individual experiences of Yorkshire, Anatolia, or Morelos. But considering what happened in sixteenth-century Songjiang should stimulate questions about how these same themes played out in other times and places.

We have also chosen documents that are particularly useful for learning *how* to analyze historical sources. Some documents are most useful for what their creators tell us about their topics: for example, a graph of trends in human energy consumption. In other documents we learn more by looking for what their creators reveal (often inadvertently) about their own assumptions, biases, and preoccupations. To take an extreme example, Adolf Hitler's writings (see *Mein Kampf* in Volume 2, Chapter 20) on Russia, Germany, and Jews tell us very little about the reality of any of those topics, but much about the obsessions of one very influential person. This document also reveals Hitler's preoccupations with struggles among

CLIMBER'S
GUIDE
TO
SOUTHERN
CALIFORNIA

Cover Photo:

Lori Ross climbing at Point Dume.

CLIMBER'S GUIDE
TO
SOUTHERN
CALIFORNIA

by

PAUL HELLWEG
and

NATHAN M. WARSTLER

ISBN 0-942568-26-5

Library of Congress Card Number 87-073435

Published in the United States of America

First Edition   1988
Second Edition   1993

Canyon Publishing Company
8561 Eatough Avenue
Canoga Park, CA 91304

SAFETY NOTICE

CLIMBING HAS
INHERENT DANGERS

SKILL, EXPERIENCE, AND MATURE JUDGEMENT
ARE THE PREREQUISITES FOR SAFE CLIMBING

NO GUIDEBOOK IS A SUBSTITUTE
FOR THESE QUALITIES

Photo courtesy of Eric Hanson

DEDICATED

to

MILT & MAXINE McAULEY

TABLE OF CONTENTS

"STONEY POINT" by Nathan Warstler, 1988

ACKNOWLEDGEMENTS

Almost invariably, authors receive help from other people in the course of completing a book. This has been particularly true with the preparation of the *Climber's Guide to Southern California*. More than four years of field research went into the project, and each of the twenty-eight sites was visited at least three times. In all these outings, the authors were typically accompanied by climbing companions who helped to rate the routes. And on many occasions, "local" climbers gave freely of their time to share knowledge of specific sites.

The authors are extremely grateful to everyone who helped, and would like to acknowledge the significant contributions made by the following individuals:

LORI LYNN ROSS — friend, climber, and professional stuntwoman — made invaluable contributions. In addition to posing for the cover photo, she furnished much site information. She also provided numerous contacts with other climbers, who subsequently were of great help.

The following friends and climbing companions accompanied the authors on field trips. They provided assistance ranging from help in rating climbs to posing for pictures. In alphabetical order, they are:

PHIL CALVERT
RUDY DeLEON
DAVE GOODALE
CHRIS HSU
SCOTT McDONALD
CRAIG McNINCH

MELANIE McNINCH
PAUL NASCHAK
MATT OLIPHANT
DAN PRESTON
KARIN SPITHORST
LAURIE ZIMMET

Four names in the above list deserve further note: PHIL CALVERT, CHRIS HSU, SCOTT McDONALD, and MATT OLIPHANT accompanied the authors on so many trips that this book could hardly have been completed without their assistance.

The following individuals provided route information on specific sites. Typically, they conducted the authors on "tours" of areas for which they were particularly knowledgeable. In alphabetical order, they are:

MICHAEL AYON   MARK TILLMAN
MATT DANCY   KEVIN VELARRLE
JEAN FRADETTE   ROGER WHITEHEAD
JAY MUELLER

In addition to all the above, the following made specific contributions as noted:

ROYAL ROBBINS — author and leading figure in the development of American climbing — contributed the Foreword.

DOUG ROBINSON contributed original poetry.

STEVE TESTERMAN assisted with some of the photography, and his friendship has been a valued source of moral support.

MILT McAULEY developed the book's format and layout.

MAXINE McAULEY did the typesetting and assisted with the layout.

It needs to be noted that MILT & MAXINE McAULEY are the editors and publishers of this book. Their support and encouragement are deeply appreciated by the authors.

Finally, two important persons need to be mentioned. KERRI WARSTLER and CATHY WILLIAMS provided the patience, understanding, encouragement, and support which were essential to the completion of this project.

To all, a hearty "thank you."

Paul Hellweg & Nathan Warstler
Northridge, CA
1988

FOREWORD

BY

Royal Robbins

When I started climbing in Southern California at age 15 a guidebook existed to only one area, Tahquitz Rock, and it was in the form of mimeographed sheets. Stoney Point was pretty much the way it is today, except the graffiti wasn't so violent, nor the broken glass so ubiquitous. Through the Rockclimbing Section of the Sierra Club we learned of other climbing sites: Pacifico, Mt. Williamson, Rubidoux, and Joshua Tree. As I look back on those days (early 1950's), I remember vividly the earnest excitement we felt as we motored out to climb at these areas (especially, of course, the incomparable Tahquitz). Climbing was a great adventure, a beacon which beckoned, a mighty magnet which drew us irresistibly towards the rocks and toward the mountains. It was the best thing going, the best possible activity. It was fresh; it was pure. We loved it because we could focus our energies 100% upon it without reservation, without fear of betrayal. It had the side benefit of fellowship. Climbers were the best people I had ever met.

Pardon me, I digress. I just wanted to say I can't wait for my next visit to Southern California so I can make use of this guidebook to visit some of the new areas which have been discovered since those early days. I like guidebooks. They enable one to make the most of the time one has available for climbing. And they enable one to more thoroughly enjoy climbs and climbing areas. They also perform other important functions, among them the setting forth for the understanding of visitors the ethics and ethos of local usage, thus helping the visitor enjoy himself without offending local sensibilities — a proper and desirable goal. The authors have in their introduction done a commendable job of covering questions of behavior and the way we treat each other. I support them and agree with what they have to say. If the reader is still in doubt, consult the Golden Rule. If that doesn't cover it, the answer can be found in one word: Charity.

Royal Robbins
Modesto, CA
1987

INTRODUCTION

Southern California is uniquely blessed with a multitude of quality climbing sites. These range from the incomparable TAHQUITZ and JOSHUA TREE to numerous relatively minor sites such as POINT MUGU and PAINTED CAVE. In between these two extremes, there are sites of virtually every size and description. The climbing ranges from bouldering to multi-pitch leading, the rock varies from friable sandstone to solid granite, and locations run the gamut from seaside to mountaintop.

The intent of the *Climber's Guide to Southern California* is to provide an overview of the available climbing in the namesake geographic region. To this end, twenty-eight rockclimbing sites are introduced in the pages that follow. These twenty-eight sites represent the best climbing that is to be found in Southern California; however, what constitutes the "best" is obviously a matter of subjective opinion. The authors visited nearly twice as many sites as are included here; those which did not make it into the text were found to be lacking in one or more essential characteristics. (The authors' Site Selection Criteria can be found enumerated later in this introduction.)

The key word in the preceding paragraph is "overview." This book makes no pretensions about being all-inclusive. Areas that are already covered by guidebooks have received lesser attention, while smaller but unguided sites are covered in greater detail. By way of example, RUBIDOUX and STONEY POINT are of approximately the same significance. But the former has twice the pages here, because a guide is not generally available. In a similar vein, TAHQUITZ, SUICIDE, and JOSHUA TREE are the premier Southern California climbing sites. However, these three sites (and many more) are covered in depth by other guidebooks. This book attempts only to introduce such sites to the first-time visitor.

SAFETY CONSIDERATIONS

A matter of paramount concern to the authors is the safety and well being of all readers. Climbing is obviously a hazardous activity, and the authors would be remiss if they were not to address the issue of safety.

All climbing is potentially dangerous, and it is not possible to cover all aspects of safety in this guide. Hence, this discussion must be limited to pointing out a few of the more obvious dangers. To begin with, rappelling has earned the reputation for being the most hazardous aspect of climbing. Problems here typically involve errors in technique, the use of unreliable anchors, and/or the lack of a proper belay. In terms of climbing in general, the most obvious hazards are rockfall from above (be cautious about following other parties), failure of protection, getting off route, attempting climbs beyond one's capabilities, and climbing unroped.

The above are by no means the only hazards. The bottom line is that each individual needs to rely on his or her own mature judgment. Each and every route should be surveyed prior to a climbing attempt — with an eye not only to the ascent, but also to the descent. Is the contemplated climb within the boundaries of your skill, experience, and equipment? If you have any doubts, be sure to provide enough protection so no uncertainty exists there. And if you wish to push your limits or take risks, you are perfectly free to do so — as long as you are mentally prepared to accept any consequences, and as long as your actions do not endanger anyone else.

Finally, one other comment needs to be made in reference to safety. This book is unique in that it discusses a large variety of climbing sites. Some are in populated urban areas. Others, however, are so remote that assistance will not be readily available. When visiting these remote sites, it is important to climb in a party of adequate size with adequate gear to be self-sufficient should an emergency arise.

STANDARDS OF CONDUCT

Royal Robbins, writing in the introduction to the *Climber's Guide to the Tahoe Region*, has divided Standards of Conduct into three categories: Personal Rules, Sporting Rules, and Community Rules. Robbins' format is followed here, with particular attention being given to Community Rules.

PERSONAL RULES

These are standards of conduct which primarily pertain to individual climbing styles. It's up to you to set your own standards. For example, will you use a bolt for protection only, or will you hang on it for aid? It doesn't really matter what style you use as long as you are honest about it (both to yourself and others), and — more importantly — you do nothing to alter the route.

SPORTING RULES: These mostly involve first ascents and are concerned with whether or not standards are to be lowered just to grab a "first." Basically, Sporting Rules primarily concern competitive climbers and thus are not within the scope of this guide.

COMMUNITY RULES: These rules concern the showing of consideration to others. An essential element is leaving the rock in exactly the same condition as you found it. This involves several factors: not placing bolts or pitons, not making any permanent modifications of the route, and limiting the use of chalk (a controversial issue, to be sure: some climbers swear by chalk; others feel it robs a route of its beauty and mystery). In short, don't deprive others of the chance to enjoy the original route.

Showing consideration to others can be a sensitive issue, especially when it comes to accepting newcomers. This book might alter climbing usage rates, and some lightly used areas might very well see increased activity. It can only be hoped that local climbers will accept the newcomers. Such acceptance has obvious rewards beyond mere good will: the opportunity to share knowledge/experiences, make friends, find new climbing partners, and so forth. Besides, through the use of this guide, climbers who frequent local sites can venture into new areas and thus become newcomers themselves.

Another significant factor effecting Community Rules is that most of the climbing sites are located on public lands. Unfortunately, public officials frequently have negative views on climbing activity. In some areas, their tolerance of climbing depends solely on the conduct of the climbers themselves. In other words, climbers who conduct themselves in an irresponsible manner may jeopardize not only their own rights but also the rights of others to use the site in the future. It is thus necessary to respect the foibles of local authorities.

In a similar vein, it is also essential for climbers to respect the rights of non-climbers. Several of the areas discussed in this book (POINT DUME, CORONA DEL MAR, etc.) are heavily used by sunbathers, hikers, picnickers, and so forth. If their rights are not respected, and/or they are exposed to danger (rockfall, etc.), the consequences may be felt by the entire climbing community. Again,

Community Rules apply: have consideration for others, whether or not they are climbers.

RATING SYSTEMS

A complete discussion of common rating systems is presented here; however, this book primarily makes use of the Yosemite Decimal System (YDS). From the outset, it must be made clear that all ratings are subjective. They are made by humans and are thus subject to human error. Also keep in mind that all ratings assume ideal conditions; darkness, rain, cold, etc. can make climbs considerably more difficult. Finally, it needs to be pointed out that ratings are subject to change. Routes can become either more or less difficult — through the intervention of nature, humans, or both.

SIERRA CLUB SYSTEM: In 1937, the Sierra Club introduced a system which divided climbing into six classes, based on increasing levels of difficulty. Briefly, the six classes are:

Class 1: Walking
Class 2: Rock scrambling
Class 3: Easy climbing; typically unroped
Class 4: Moderate climbing; typically roped
Class 5: Difficult climbing; rope and protection required.
Class 6: Aid climbing

Virtually all routes in this book are Class 5. Class 1 - 4 are occasionally mentioned in reference to an approach or descent; Class 6 climbs are rarely included.

YOSEMITE DECIMAL SYSTEM (YDS): This system was developed at TAHQUITZ in the 1950's, but was popularized at YOSEMITE (hence its name). The YDS uses a decimal system to subdivide Class 5 climbs. Ratings range from 5.0 for the easiest to 5.14 for the most severe. To put this system into perspective, climbs of 5.0 to 5.5 are typically suitable for beginners (providing adequate protection is available), climbs of 5.6 to 5.9 are of intermediate difficulty, and climbs of 5.10 and up are generally for the highly skilled (5.12 has been compared to climbing a "vertical pane of glass"). There are no 5.13 or 5.14 climbs in this book; such climbs are for those on the leading edge of standard setting.

16

For many years, the YDS topped out at 5.10, and it was a long time before 5.11 was accepted as a general standard. As a result, most climbers feel that 5.10 covers too large a range of difficulty. It is thus common to further subdivide 5.10 into four categories, 5.10A - 5.10D ("A" being the easiest; "D" being the hardest). Likewise, climbs of 5.11 and above are also subdivided into the A - D categories.

This guidebook uses the YDS ratings with one notable exception. Unless there is a great deal of consensus (such as at MOUNT WOODSON), the A - D subdivisions are not employed. Instead, all climbs higher than the "B" rating are denoted by a plus (+) sign.

GRADE RATINGS: Roman numerals are frequently used to grade the overall difficulty of a climb; however, in common usage, the Grade Rating typically refers to the length of time required to complete a route. Some discrepancy exists on Grade Ratings, but a common standard can be found in the classic text, *Mountaineering: the Freedom of the Hills.* This standard is used here:

Grade	I:	Several hours (or less)
Grade	II:	Half a day
Grade	III:	Most of a day
Grade	IV:	Long hard day
Grade	V:	1½ - 2½ days
Grade	VI:	More than 2 days

Grade Ratings are not employed in this text. Instead, the number of pitches are given for longer routes. Generally speaking, climbs of three pitches or less are Grade I — and this accounts for the vast majority of routes included herein. Rarely will climbs of Grades III or IV be encountered, though there are climbs of up to eight pitches at TAHQUITZ. Inexperienced climbers have been known to spend a night on TAHQUITZ, but — technically speaking — there are no Grade V or VI climbs in this book.

AID RATINGS: Aid climbing is defined as the use of anything other than natural features for assistance while climbing. There are very few aid climbs in this book; however, for the sake of completeness, Aid Ratings are described:

A1: Easy and secure placements
A2: Difficult, but secure placements

A3: Difficult placements, will hold only a short fall
A4: Difficult placements, will hold body weight but
     not a fall
A5: Thirty or more feet of continuous A4 placements

POISON OAK

All Southern California climbers should be familiar with this plant: It is found at approximately half the rockclimbing sites discussed in this book. Poison Oak is a woody shrub or vine that causes dermatitis upon contact with its leaves, flowers, fruits, and bark. Though some persons claim immunity, recent research suggests that susceptibility is a matter of degree. Everyone should thus learn to identify and avoid this plant.

Poison Oak is best identified by its leaves. These are alternate and compound, with each leaf having three distinct leaflets. The leaves are shiny green on top, but will turn red in the Fall. Poison Oak is most commonly found in moist and shady areas — such as on slopes of northern exposure.

If you make actual or suspected contact with this plant, wash the effected area with plenty of hot water and detergent (either laundry or dishwashing). The allergenic agent is an oil based resin. Ordinary hand soaps do a poor job of removing this oil; likely they'd only spread it around. Washing will be reasonably effective if conducted within twelve hours of exposure; however, the sooner done, the better.

RATTLESNAKES

Rattlesnakes might be encountered at virtually all the sites in this book. Rattlesnakes are identified by their triangular-shaped heads and comparatively thick bodies. In contrast, non-poisonous snakes in Southern California tend to have oval heads and slender bodies.

In order to reduce the likelihood of a bite, be alert to the possible presence of a snake. Rattlesnakes — like all other reptiles — cannot internally regulate their body temperature. They are thus typically found in the shade on hot days, but in the sun on cool days. Also, it is important to note that the vast majority of bites occur when individuals attempt to kill or capture a snake. If the snake is left alone, the chances of a bite are drastically reduced.

This is not the place to get into a detailed discussion of snakebite first aid. Just keep in mind that the best possible course of action is to seek immediate professional medical assistance. And if you're venturing into remote areas where help will not be readily available, it would be wise to carry a snakebite kit and to be familiar with its use.

SITE SELECTION CRITERIA

To conclude this introduction, the authors would like to point out the standards used in deciding which sites to include in the text. As has been mentioned, numerous sites have not been included because they failed to meet the following requirements. This set of guidelines is obviously highly subjective, but a brief perusal will nonetheless better help the reader understand the intended scope of this book.

GEOGRAPHIC SETTING: The geographic area covered is Southern California, starting at a point just north of Santa Barbara and running south to the Mexican border. Primary attention is given to sites that are readily accessible to climbers living in (or visiting) the coastal metropolitan region which extends almost continuously from Santa Barbara to San Diego.

POPULARITY: This book covers only rockclimbing sites that are already reasonably established. No attempt has been made to develop new climbing areas.

ACCESS: Ease of access was a major selection criterion. The amount and quality of the climbing needed to be proportional to the effort required to reach the site. Areas that require a long drive, an arduous hike, or both (such as TAHQUITZ) are included only if the climbing is good enough — which, of course is the case at TAHQUITZ. But numerous sites did not meet this criterion. UPPER GIBRALTAR, as an example, requires bushwhacking and scrambling to reach a rock that has only three established routes. Thus UPPER GIBRALTAR (and similar sites) did not make it into the text.

AESTHETIC APPEAL: This was by far the most subjective criterion. Generally speaking, a site needed something to recommend it. Typically this would be the quality of the climbing; however, occasionally the setting was also taken into consideration. Thus sites like POINT MUGU are included. (POINT MUGU has only one boulder, but its seaside setting adds greatly to its appeal.)

LEGALITY: Sites where climbing is prohibited are not included herein. By way of example, DEERHORN VALLEY is considered by some to be the premier San Diego site. The area, however, is on private land and is conspicuously marked with "No trespassing" signs. DEERHORN VALLEY is accordingly not included. At the time of this writing, climbing is tolerated at all sites presented in this book. This does not mean to imply that climbing is encouraged or even officially condoned. Furthermore, tolerance can be a fleeting phenomena. If any doubt exists, climbers should consult with local authorities.

Now that the scope of this book is understood, all that remains is to enjoy the climbing. It's unlikely that many climbers will have previously visited all 28 sites; thus, there should be something for everyone. The authors sincerely hope the *Climber's Guide to Southern California* proves to be a source for safe and rewarding climbing experiences.

Introduction to Second Edition
A lot has changed since this book was first published five years ago. New areas have been developed, and older areas that had previously received little attention have become popular sites. All of this increased climbing activity has been mirrored in an increase in the available literature. When this book came out, it was the only one of its kind. Today there are several guidebooks that are devoted to the Southern California climbing scene. None of this, however, changes the basic intent of this book, which is to: provide an overview of the available climbing, furnish sufficient information for a first visit, and then refer readers to sources of more detailed information.

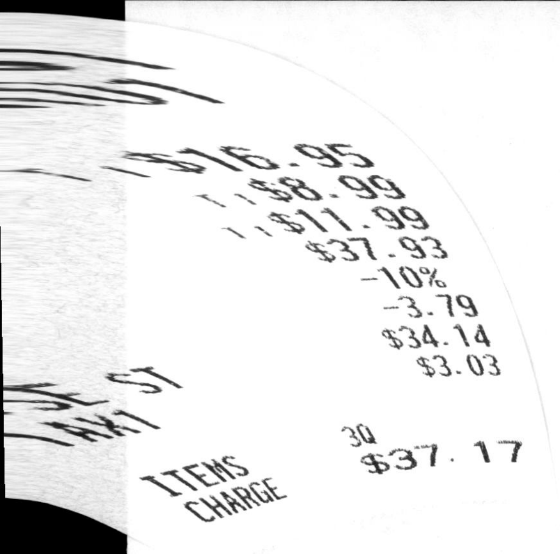

$16.95
$8.99
$11.99
$37.93
-10%
-3.79
$34.14
$3.03

SL ST
AX1

ITEMS
CHARGE

3Q
$37.17

THE CLIMBING SITES

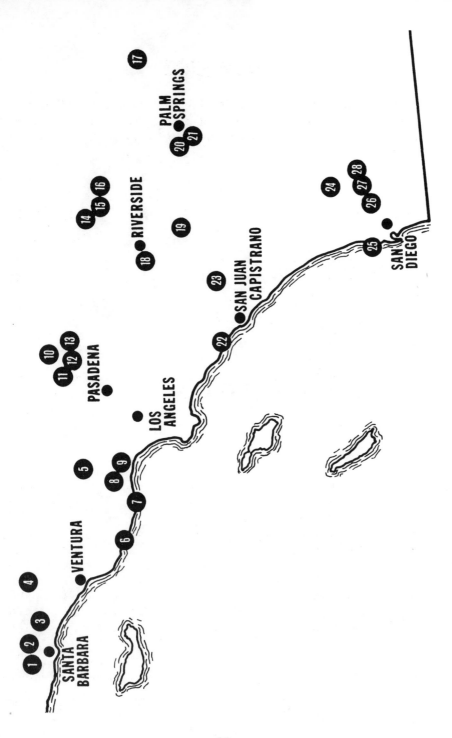

SANTA BARBARA

VENTURA

PASADENA

LOS ANGELES

RIVERSIDE

PALM SPRINGS

SAN JUAN CAPISTRANO

SAN DIEGO

Climbing areas are pre... the northwest and working down and rig... the arrangement is geographic, a site's order of... reflection on its overall quality.

1 PAINTED CAVE

Painted Cave Boulder As Seen From The Parking Area

PAINTED CAVE is Santa Barbara's most popular bouldering site. It's quite small — the primary climbing area consists of only two large boulders plus one smaller rock. However, the three have classic qualities. On the right side of the road (as seen driving up), there is an alcove with a prominent overhang. There are good holds here, and they provide ample opportunity for some strenuous pump-outs. The same boulder has good face climbing problems, some of which are steep and exposed. On the opposite side of the road, the large boulder which leans out over the pavement also has an abundance of classic problems. One of the best is the exposed route which ascends a series of small holes up the middle of the face shown in the photo above. Elsewhere, the climbing consists of fun traverses and decent mantles.

PAINTED CAVE draws its name from a Chumash pictograph site located about half a mile further up the road. The Indian site has historical interest, and it's worth the short drive or walk required to see it.

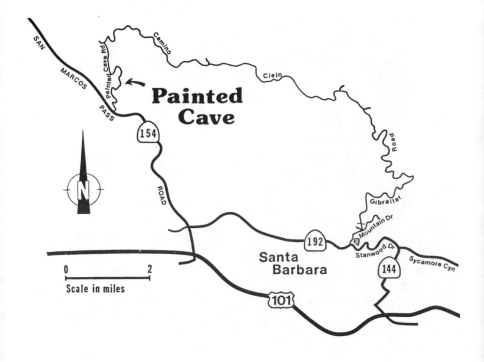

DIRECTIONS

Near the northern edge of the city of Santa Barbara, exit 101 onto Route 154 and head north towards the mountains. Take 154 approximately 5½ miles to Painted Cave Road. Stay alert: this intersection appears with very little advance warning. Turn right onto Painted Cave and follow the winding road one and a half miles. The climbing area will appear as two large boulders, one on each side of the road. Parking is just past the boulder on the right.

2

GIBRALTAR ROCK

GIBRALTAR ROCK is the single most popular climbing site in the entire Santa Barbara area. This is due to several factors: it offers a variety of excellent routes of up to 150 feet in length, it's located right next to the road and is thus readily accessible, and most of the routes can be top-roped. Though the climbing area can get quite hot, there are frequently refreshing breezes and/or coastal overcast, either of which can make climbing conditions very pleasant indeed. On the other hand, if the day should happen to be clear, the summit of Gibraltar offers magnificent panoramic views of the Pacific Ocean and Channel Islands. All in all, GIBRALTAR ROCK is a great place to climb, and it's well worth the long drive for those coming from Los Angeles or other distant areas.

GIBRALTAR ROCK has two main climbing faces, which are the South and West faces respectively. All South Face routes and a couple West Face routes are described here. For information on other climbs, consult Steve Tucker's guidebook, *Climbing in Santa Barbara and Ventura Counties.* It should also be noted that there are numerous other climbing sites in the general Gibraltar area. These include Hole-In-The-Rock Boulder and the Bolt Ladder, both of which are described herein. Other nearby sites include Upper & Lower Gibraltar Rocks, Cold Springs Dome, and Cathedral Peak. These latter sites are not discussed primarily because they are either of lesser quality or access is much more difficult. But they are included in Tucker's book. Again, this guide should be consulted for additional information.

Getting back to GIBRALTAR ROCK itself, the South Face routes can be reached by an obvious path which leads to the base of the climbs. Other paths lead to the summit, where good bolts can be found for top-rope belays. Most of the routes can also be lead; however, protection is typically pretty sparse on the upper sections.

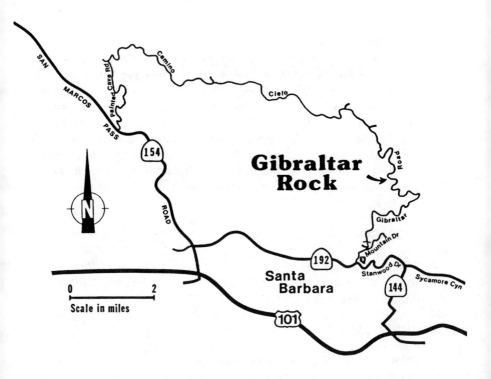

DIRECTIONS

From Highway 101, exit onto Milpas Street and head inland into Santa Barbara. Follow Route 144 by turning right onto Mason Street, left on Salinas Street and right on Sycamore Canyon Road. At the intersection with Route 192 (Stanwood Drive), turn left. Watch for Sheffield Reservoir on the right. Mountain Drive will appear just past the reservoir—turn right onto Mountain. Approximately 1/4 mile up Mountain, turn onto Gibraltar Road, which is the middle street of a three-way intersection. Continue on Gibraltar Road past an intersection with El Cielito, and relax—the difficult direction-finding is over. GIBRALTAR ROCK will appear on the left side of the road about 4½ miles past the El Cielito intersection.

CLIMBING ROUTES

1. ANY MINUTE NOW   5.6

This is primarily a West Face route; however, the start is visible in the South Face photo. Ascend the obvious crack/flake underneath the left edge of the southwest corner's prominent overhang. Climb up and left to a corner block. Above the corner (bolted), ascend a short ramp up and left into a slanting corner, which leads to a wide ledge (the Peanut Gallery). From the ledge, hand traverse the crack which angles up and right to an alcove. The chimney above leads to the top.

2. T-CRACK   5.10

This is another West Face Route. From the sloping ramp of route #1, ascend the difficult crack up and right. Numerous variations are possible above.

3. THE NOSE   5.10+

Start in the crack below the prominent overhang of the southwest corner. Once the overhang is passed, continue following the same crack to a small grassy ledge. From here, unprotected face climbing leads to the top.

4. KLINGON   5.8

Start in the southwest corner, but bypass the overhang by ascending a left-facing open book. Continue in the open book as it angles up and right, where a block is passed (on the left) to reach the grassy ledge. Continue straight up face to reach the top.

5. MID-FACE   5.6

Ascend the thin crack near the middle of the South Face. When the crack disappears, easier face climbing leads to the top.

SOUTH FACE ROUTES

6.   THE LADDER   5.5

Climb the obvious crack at the right-hand base of the South Face. The crux is the bulge found at the second ledge. For an easier variation (5.1), the bulge can be bypassed by traversing to another crack a few feet to the right.

*Laurie Zimmet on the top portion of
the Mid-Face Route*

MISCELLANEOUS CLIMBING AREAS

THE BOLT LADDER

The Bolt Ladder is located approximately 150 yards down the road from GIBRALTAR ROCK (on the left-hand side, as seen walking back from the parking turnouts). The bolts are closely spaced together, thus providing a good opportunity for beginners to practice aid technique. The route can also be done free, but this is quite difficult (5.11).

HOLE-IN-THE-ROCK BOULDER

This boulder is located on the hillside just across the road from GIBRALTAR ROCK proper. It's easily identified by the namesake hole on its west face (that is, the side facing Gibraltar). Hole-In-The-Rock is a popular top-roping site, and there are routes on the north, west, and south faces. A popular climb goes up the right-hand side of the west face. Three variations are possible; all start with a climb into the above-mentioned hole. From this hole, either go up using corner holds (5.7); go straight to the top without using the corner (5.9); or traverse up and left (5.10+). There are bolts at the top for belaying.

3

SAN YSIDRO

SAN YSIDRO is a picturesque mountain canyon located in Montecito just south of the city of Santa Barbara. The canyon contains two climbing walls, the lower of which is more readily accessible (the upper wall requires an additional mile and a half of uphill hiking). The lower wall is accordingly more popular and is the one described herein. It's composed of high-quality sandstone, and — at its highest — is about 200 feet tall.

SAN YSIDRO is primarily a lead-climbing site. A few of the routes can be top-roped, but all can be (and typically are) lead. All routes are protected by bolts; however, the lead-outs are occasionally quite long. It's thus helpful to bring along a small selection of chocks.

To reach the lower climbing wall, hike up the maintained trail from the parking area. This trail heads uphill through a residential area, briefly skirts a paved road, then turns into a fire road. Continue up the fire road until the climbing formation can be seen to the left. At this point, any of a variety of scrambleways lead down and across a creek, then on to the base of the rock. Be very careful, as there is an abundance of poison oak in the area — both along the maintained trail and especially along the scrambleways.

San Ysidro Canyon

Scale in miles
0   1

East Mountain Dr

Park Lane

Rd

East Valley

192

MONTECITO

San Ysidro Road

N

101

DIRECTIONS

Exit the 101 Freeway onto San Ysidro Road just south of the Santa Barbara city limits. Turn inland towards the mountains and proceed slightly less than one mile to East Valley Road (Route 192). Turn right, and again proceed slightly less than one mile to Park Lane. Turn left onto Park Lane, then left again onto East Mountain Drive. The trailhead is on the right about 1/4 mile up East Mountain Drive.

CLIMBING ROUTES

1. **VANISHING FLAKES**   5.10+

On the left-hand side of the main climbing formation, ascend to a fixed pin at an undercling. Exit to the face above and angle right about 10 feet to a bolt. Head straight up from here, exiting via the large crack above.

2. **ROCKOCCO**   5.7

Ascend the right-facing corner (about 15 feet to the right of route #1). Follow this corner as it angles up and left to join route #1.

3. **FACE LIFT**   5.7

About 35 feet right of route #2, there is a large triangular flake at the base of the rock. Ascend the right edge of this flake to reach a bolt above. Continue up and right past several bolts to reach a two-bolt belay. Exit up and left.

Variations

a.   (5.10)   Climb the face protected by a bolt just left of the start described above.

b.   (5.9)   From the belay bolts, follow further bolts up and right. At the highest bolt, traverse right to a short & steep face, which is climbed straight up (protected by one last bolt).

4. **GREAT RACE**   5.9

Near the center of the climbing formation, scramble about 40 feet up the 3rd class gully to reach a bushy ledge. The climb starts here. Ascend the steep face above, following the line of four bolts.

5. PEELS OF LAUGHTER 5.6

Ascend the notched and pocketed prow immediately to the right of the central gully. Stay pretty much on the corner all the way up. Protected by two bolts, but has a long run-out to the first.

6. MANY HAPPY RETURNS 5.9

Ascend a smooth face to a bolt (about 10 feet to the right of route #5). Continue up and right to a second bolt, which protects a difficult left-facing lieback. Above the lieback, follow the obvious crack past two more bolts.

7. RICK'S ROUTE 5.7

Head up the base of the rock to the right of route #6. At a point about 15 feet to the right of a large and prominent bulge, there is a smaller bulge (protected by a bolt). The route goes up and over this smaller bulge, then follows the trough above.

4

SESPE GORGE

SESPE GORGE offers the best multi-pitch lead climbing that is readily accessible from the greater Los Angeles/Ventura metropolitan area (it is approximately a 2½ hour drive from the San Fernando Valley, much less from Santa Barbara or Ventura). The main wall of the Gorge extends to over 300 feet in height, and numerous crack systems provide for excellent climbing. Steve Tucker's Santa Barbara guide lists a total of twenty-one routes, enough to fill several climbing days. The five routes listed here are among the best, and they provide a rather decent introduction to this site.

The rock is fine-grained and solid sandstone; however, some of the routes have loose rock and care needs to be exercised to ensure the safety of both climber and belayer. All routes begin from the streambed at the foot of the wall; the stream is typically low enough to not interfere with access to the climbs.

DESCENT

Three options exist for descending the main wall. There is a fourth-class gully (behind the water station platform) which provides a popular, though somewhat risky descent (there is much loose rock). A safer but more tedious downclimb involves a roundabout route: climb up and over broken rock to the left of the fourth-class gully, then descend via the left backside of the wall. Finally, if two full-length ropes are available, a rappel to the streambed may be made from the top of the climb known as the "Pipe Route."

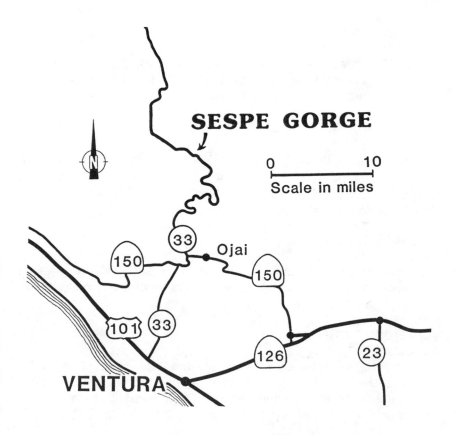

DIRECTIONS (from Los Angeles)

Take the 101 Freeway north through Ventura and exit onto the Ojai Freeway (route 33). Continue north on 33 and turn right (east) on 150 (Baldwin Road). After approximately 1.5 miles, turn left back onto Highway 33. Exactly 20 miles from this intersection, Sespe Gorge will appear as the very obvious sandstone wall on the left. The best parking is on the shoulder of the west (left) side — be sure to park well off the road since Highway 33 has comparatively heavy traffic.

MAIN WALL CLIMBING ROUTES

1. PIPE PRIME   5.6

PIPE PRIME starts from the obvious crack a few feet to the left of the PIPE ROUTE (see below). Follow the crack directly to the fourth-class gully. (One pitch.)

2. PIPE ROUTE   5.6

An obvious crack ascends straight up the wall from the point where a pipe is attached (about 50 feet right of the steel platform). Follow the crack directly to the fourth-class gully above. (One very long pitch.)

3. PIPE CLEANER   5.6

Ascend the thin crack to the right of PIPE ROUTE. Climb terminates in a notch adjacent to the fourth-class gully. (Two pitches.)

4. ENDING CRACK   5.7

Ascend the obvious straight crack to the right of the PIPE CLEANER. The crack ends near the top (thus the climb's name). To finish, climb the face (unprotected) straight up, or traverse right and up to the ending point of the TREE LINE. (Two or three pitches.)

5. TREE LINE   5.5

Follow the obvious crack to the left of the large pinetree. Belay from the first tree, one full pitch straight-up. Then proceed up and left to a second belay tree. One short pitch remains, straight up to the ending notch. (Three pitches.)

MAIN WALL CLIMBING ROUTES

5

STONEY POINT

STONEY POINT is a city park located in the suburbs of Los Angeles, and it is the major climbing site within the entire L.A. metropolitan region. Though its land area is small (only 22 acres), its sandstone bluffs and boulders are extensively climbed. There are some limited opportunities for lead and direct-aid climbing; however, STONEY POINT is primarily a top-roping and bouldering site. In such capacity, it excels. It has at least a dozen large faces, all of which are climbable. And there's seemingly no limit to its bouldering potential: its slopes are covered with large and climbable boulders and outcrops.

In addition to its diversified climbing opportunities, STONEY POINT is noteworthy from a historical point of view (climbing history, that is). The names of many well-known climbing personalities are closely associated with STONEY POINT. Royal Robbins and Yvon Chouinard, for example, both got their start at Stoney.

For more detailed information on both climbing history and climbing opportunities, consult the *Stoney Point Guide* by Paul Hellweg and Don Fisher. The book is readily available in local mountaineering shops. In the meantime, the following pages introduce the newcomer to both bouldering and top-roping sites at Stoney.

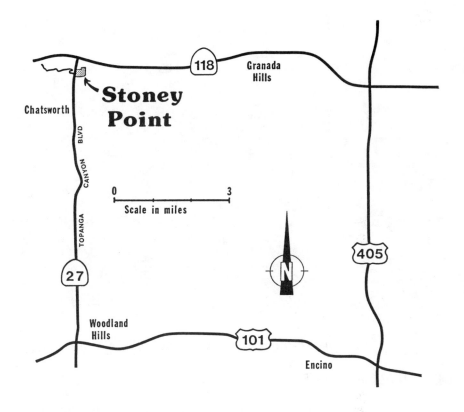

DIRECTIONS

Take the Simi Valley Freeway (118) west and exit at Topanga Canyon Boulevard. Turn left onto Topanga and head south about 1/2 mile — Stoney Point is the unmistakable rock upthrust on the left. Alternately, Topanga Canyon Boulevard is accessible from the Ventura Freeway (101). Take Topanga north to a point just past the turnoff for Santa Susana Pass Road.

A dirt driveway runs down into Stoney Point Park, but it is not open to vehicular traffic. Park on the east side of Topanga Canyon Boulevard, and walk down the slight incline to the climbing sites.

OVERVIEW — Stoney Point from the southwest

BOULDERING

As mentioned before, Stoney Point is a preeminent bouldering site. The place to start is "Slant Rock" (visible in the lower right foreground of the overview photo). Its sloping west face is ideal for practicing balance, and many climbers use it for "warming-up" exercises. For a challenge, try climbing this face by balance alone; that is, without using your hands. Slant Rock's north side offers a variety of additional bouldering problems — including good mantles and laybacks.

Next stop is Boulder I (visible in lower left foreground of the overview photo). One of the more popular problems here is a traverse of the boulder's entire circumference. Start in the dihedral at the northeast corner and work in a clockwise direction. Don't get discouraged if you do not succeed in making the complete traverse; portions of it are 5.11+. Boulder I also has several top-rope climbs. The anchoring bolt on top can be reached by climbing the easy (5.1) east face.

For additional bouldering opportunities, walk down the dirt road which heads east from Stoney Point's main entrance off Topanga Canyon Boulevard. Several good sites are found along this road. Angel's Wing (a.k.a. the Pile-ups) is about half-way to Stoney's southeast corner; an incredibly strenuous hand and arm traverse runs across the side facing the dirt road. At Stoney's southeast corner proper, there are several more good boulders — the largest of which is Boulder II (a.k.a. Turlock). Like Boulder I, Boulder II offers both bouldering and top-roping opportunities. Head up the "Stairs" on the southwest corner to reach anchoring bolts on top.

Craig McNinch climbing the chimney at Split Rock (a boulder which makes a useful landmark for finding Backwall climbing routes).

TOP-ROPING

The *Stoney Point Guide* describes a total of 55 top-roped climbs, many of which are on the previously-mentioned Boulders I & II. In addition, the guide discusses twelve other top-roping sites, two of which are introduced on the following pages.

THE BEEHIVE

THE BEEHIVE and BEETHOVEN'S WALL (see page after next) together form Stoney Point's northeast corner. The rock is about sixty feet high, which — though it may not sound too impressive — is nonetheless among the highest at Stoney. The routes are all high quality, and there's something for everyone; the climbing ranges in difficulty from 5.4 to 5.11.

As THE BEEHIVE'S name implies, there are in fact hives in the area. The bees typically do not bother climbers; however, anyone allergic to their stings should take suitable precautions.

To reach Stoney's northeast corner, follow the dirt driveway east from Topanga Canyon Boulevard. Continue on this road as it swings north and passes "Split Rock" (an obviously split boulder visible on the left). At this point, various scrambleways lead up and right to THE BEEHIVE and BEETHOVEN'S WALL.

Access to the top is by way of a canyon around the corner to the northwest. At the top, there are several good-sized boulders conveniently positioned for use as anchors.

ROUTES

1.   **BLACK'S CRACK**   **5.7**
Start either in the crack or on the face to its immediate right. The crack is at first vertical, but soon changes to a slope of lesser exposure — the crux occurs at just this point where the climb changes angle.

2.   **TELEPHONE BOOTH**   **5.10+**
Start from a small alcove a few feet to the right of Black's Crack. Bridge the alcove's side walls to reach holds high and to the right, then use these holds to work up to a small slab. This is the end of the hard part — the path upwards follows the Beehive route (see #3, below).

3.   **BEEHIVE**   **5.4**
Start in the chimney, work up the slab, and continue to the corner above (where one encounters a tricky squeeze to reach the top). The Beehive is a classic, and it's probably the best climb at Stoney Point for beginners.

THE BEEHIVE

BEETHOVEN'S WALL

BEETHOVEN'S WALL is the most popular climbing "wall" at Stoney Point. It offers classic high-angle face climbing, and its routes appeal to both intermediate and advanced climbers. The face can be climbed almost anywhere. Of all the variations attempted, only the five best (and most obvious) are described here.

For directions, refer to The Beehive (preceding pages); BEETHOVEN'S wall is immediately around the corner from the Beehive. Access to the top is by way of a canyon just right of the face. At the top, there's a large boulder perfectly situated for use as an anchor. Either place long runners around this boulder, or slot chocks underneath it.

CAUTION: There's a little bit of poison oak near the bottom of BEETHOVEN'S WALL.

ROUTES

1. **THE PROW**   5.11
   Head straight up the left corner of Beethoven's Wall.

2. **FACE**   5.9
   Head pretty much straight up the face to the right of The Prow (route #1, above). The holds are thin, few, and far apart.

3. **FACE**   5.10
   This route starts from the center, swings right, then heads back left to end almost directly above where it started.

4. **FACE**   5.7
   Follow the large crack to its end, then move out onto the face. Traverse right and up to a short flaring crack which gives access to the top.

5. **FACE**   5.7
   Mantle up onto a narrow ledge, then traverse left and up to the top of the large crack. From here, the route is the same as #4 above.

BEETHOVEN'S WALL

6

POINT MUGU

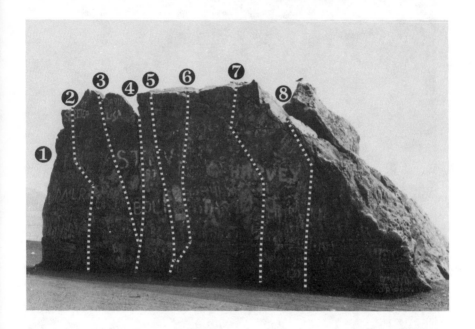

The climbing at POINT MUGU consists of just one solitary boulder. However, it's a classic, and it has become quite popular. The boulder is approximately 20 feet high, and its north face has more than half-a-dozen exceptionally fine cracks. This face is slightly overhanging, thus the cracks tend to be difficult — all are 5.8 or harder. Several bolts have been placed on top, but virtually all have been chopped. It's thus advisable to bring along a couple of medium-sized chocks to help in establishing a safe belay.

The boulder sits on a point of land which juts out into the Pacific Ocean. This combination of seaside setting and classic cracks accounts for POINT MUGU'S popularity, and the site is highly recommended for anyone desiring to work on his or her crack technique.

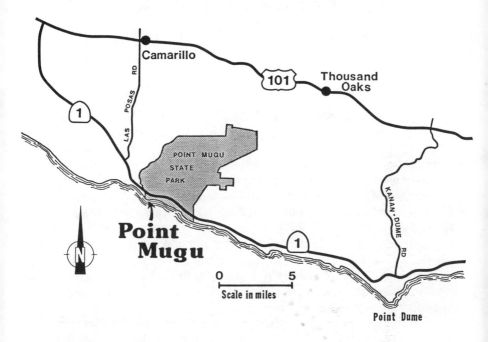

DIRECTIONS

Point Mugu lies along the Pacific Coast Highway (Route 1) between Oxnard and Malibu. A good landmark to look for is the Point Mugu Naval Station's firing range — the climbing rock is located slightly south of the range. There's a large parking turnout on the west (ocean) side of the highway immediately adjacent to the Point Mugu boulder.

Route Ratings:

1. 5.9 (edge)
2. 5.9
3. 5.9
4. 5.9
5. 5.9
6. 5.10
7. 5.10
8. 5.8

7

POINT DUME

The climbing site at POINT DUME is the 50 foot high sea bluff at the southern edge of Zuma State Beach. This bluff has excellent climbing potential: the holds are sound, and the face can be climbed most anywhere. Of all the variations possible, only the three most obvious routes are described in the following pages.

POINT DUME'S proximity to Zuma Beach is a mixed blessing. On the one hand, the ocean setting has obvious advantages. In fact, the magnificence of the surrounding seascape is the site's primary attraction. Cool ocean breezes, panoramic vistas, and the pounding surf below — all these make for an ideal climbing environment. And if that is not enough, the adjacent beaches are among Southern California's finest. This last point, however, can work to the climber's disadvantage.

Zuma Beach is quite popular, and on a hot summer weekend it is typically packed with sunbathers. Overcrowding causes lots of problems, not the least of which is that parking space becomes difficult to find. A more serious problem involves the sunbathers themselves. Local authorities tolerate climbing activity, but they insist that climbers do not inconvenience or, worse, endanger other beach users. The problem is that the beach can get crowded right up to the base of the climbing bluff. On such days, climbing activity could potentially endanger others (thrown ropes, dropped equipment, rockfall, and so forth). In order to avoid potential problems, POINT DUME is best climbed on days when sunbathers are not present en masse. And at all times, climbers should be mindful that their activities might be a source of concern to others.

The preceding comments have not been intended to discourage climbing at POINT DUME. As mentioned above, the climbing is good and the setting is superb. Just be responsible in your activities, and all parties can have a rewarding day.

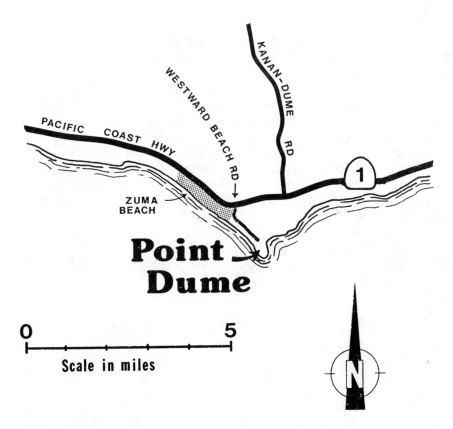

DIRECTIONS

Point Dume is located on the southern edge of Zuma State Beach. Exit the Pacific Coast Highway (Route 1) at Westward Beach Road, approximately one mile north of Malibu. This is a left-hand turn for those coming from the direction of Malibu, and the turnoff appears just south of the main entrance to Zuma Beach. Follow Westward Beach Road as it curves south, and park at the end of the road. Point Dume is the obvious sea bluff just ahead.

A fee is required to park at the road end as mentioned above. If the pay lot is full — or if one desires to avoid the parking fee — then make use of the limited parking available along Westward Beach Road. It's about a 3/4 mile walk from the fee station to the climbing site.

CLIMBING ROUTES

There are five bolted climbing routes on Point Dume's northwest face. The original hangers are badly rusted, but many have been replaced with newer bolts that seem to be suitable for leading. But some climbers may prefer to utilize a top-rope belay. To set up a top belay, take the obvious path which leads to the summit. On the top, there's a solid rock which can be looped with webbing to serve as an anchor. Be sure to take along several yards of webbing for this purpose.

1. FACE, LEFT   5.9
   Follow the left-most line of bolts, then traverse right to join route #2.

2. FACE   5.8
   Follow line of bolts that angles up and slightly right.

3. FACE, CENTER   5.8
   Follow center line of bolts up and slightly right.

4. FACE, RIGHT   5.7
   Follow bolts up and slightly left.

5. ARETE   5.6
   Start near outside corner. Climb either straight up, or veer slightly right to make use of corner holds.

6. WEST FACE   5.10 (Not pictured)
   This climb is located around the corner from Route #5, on the side of the bluff facing the ocean. Climb up broken rock to a crack left of prominent overhang, traverse right to crack immediately below overhang, then exit up and right. Top rope.

POINT DUME

8

ROCK POOL
"LITTLE EUROPE"

Unbeknownst to the authors at the time the original 1988 edition of this book was published, LITTLE EUROPE is a long-established site. However, the climbing potential was a closely-guarded secret known only to a handful of local climbers. The situation has changed since then, and at least three guidebooks now offer detailed descriptions of the climbing: Fry's *Southern California Bouldering Guide,* Katz's *Getting High in L.A.,* and Mayr's *Sport Crags in Southern California.* Because so much information is in print elsewhere, this section has not been expanded. The intent here, as elsewhere, is merely to serve as an introduction to the area.

The narrow gorge upstream from the namesake ROCK POOL has an abundance of both bouldering and climbing routes. The area is primarily an attraction for experienced climbers because the routes are mostly 5.10 and harder; also, the bouldering problems rarely have safe landing areas. Nevertheless, LITTLE EUROPE does appeal to less experienced climbers. The site is quite scenic, there are frequently refreshing breezes and lots of shade, and it's usually possible to take a post-workout dip in the pool (depending on the season and amount of water, the pool ranges from brimful to a nearly dried-up puddle).

Furthermore, the PLANET OF THE APES WALL offers excellent rappelling opportunities. It should be noted, however, that State Park Rangers discourage rappelling elsewhere. Also, Rangers discourage the placement of new bolts; it is their stated policy to chop all bolts immediately upon discovery.

DIRECTIONS

Malibu Creek State Park is located along Las Virgenes Road (aka Malibu Canyon). To get to the park, exit the Ventura Freeway at Las Virgenes and head south. In about 3¼ miles, the road crosses Mulholland Highway. Be alert; the entrance to the park comes up fast — it's on the right about 2/10ths of a mile past Mulholland. The State Park is a fee area, so you'll need to bring along a few dollars to get in.

It should be noted that Malibu Creek State Park is subject to fire closures. These can occur at any time of the year, but are especially frequent from August to November. It thus might be wise to phone ahead for closure information. Call either (213) 454-2372 for a recorded message, or call the Park Headquarters at (818) 706-8809. When there's no fire closure, the park is open from 8 a.m. till sunset.

*Rock Pool's namesake pool —
bouldering area is beyond water.*

CLIMBING NOTES

To reach ROCK POOL, hike the road/trail to the Visitor's Center. This starts from the southwest corner of the parking area, and it's slightly over 3/4th of a mile to the Visitor's Center. From there, cross the bridge over Malibu Creek and take the "Gorge Trail" which is found just past the bridge. Hike upstream for about 1/4 mile to reach ROCK POOL. PLANET OF THE APES WALL is on the right-hand side just before reaching the pool. It has an easy walk-up on the downstream side and good anchors on top.

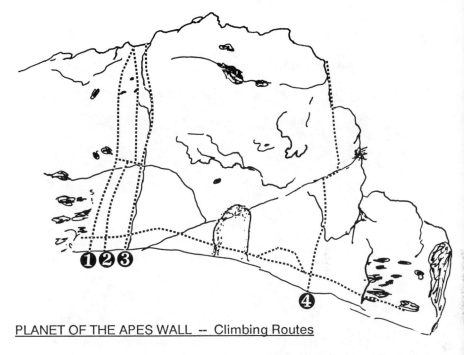

PLANET OF THE APES WALL -- Climbing Routes

The overhanging wall has four established top-rope climbs. In addition, there is a low traverse (PLANET OF THE APES TRAVERSE, 5.11+) that runs the entire width of the rock.

1. SPIDER MONKEY		5.11+
2. FINGER PRINTS		5.11+
3. PLANET OF THE APES (direct finish)		5.11+
4. WALKING ON THE MOON		5.11+

ADDITIONAL CLIMBING

To reach the main climbing/bouldering areas, proceed upstream past ROCK POOL. The route scrambles up the west (right-hand) embankment, then drops down close to the water. At this point, an entertaining traverse leads to the climbing areas beyond. One of the first features reached is a large rock "cave," the interior of which provides a difficult overhanging traverse (5.12). Refer to the aforementioned guidebooks (see page 54) for additional route information.

9

PURPLE STONES

Two of the principal climbing boulders, Purple Stones.

PURPLE STONES is a bouldering area located in the canyon of Topanga Creek, not far from the Pacific Ocean. It is an idyllic place to climb: the creek flows year-round, there's lots of shade in the canyon bottom, and the boulders -- though few in number -- are of high quality. The rocks are of good size and are formed of a reasonably sound sandstone conglomerate, which provides surprisingly good holds. Accordingly, some nice routes have been established. Most of these routes tend to be difficult (5.10 and up), but there are ample opportunities for finding easier problems. Though the climbing is technically bouldering, many of the routes are done top-roped because landings tend to be hazardous.

It's not necessary to know the established routes to enjoy an afternoon of bouldering, but for those who are interested, detailed descriptions can be found in Fry's *Southern California Bouldering Guide* and Katz's *Getting High in L.A.*

There is a parking turnout adjacent to the scrambleway that leads to the boulders. But it is illegal to park there, thus the directions on the next page recommend an alternative approach.

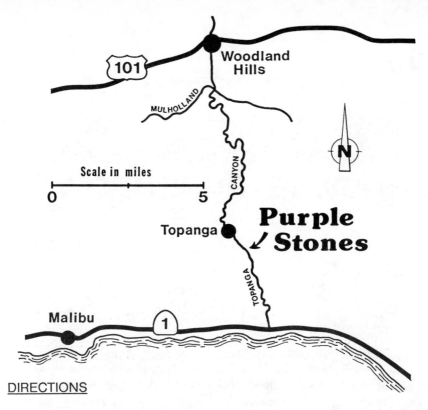

DIRECTIONS

PURPLE STONES is located along Topanga Canyon approximately one half mile south of the town of Topanga. Topanga Canyon can be reached off the Ventura Freeway from the north, or off the Pacific Coast Highway from the south. If coming from the north, look for the following prominent sign: "NO PARKING ANY TIME NEXT 1½ MILES." This sign is located at the southern edge of the town. Park just before the sign and walk (very, very carefully) down Topanga Canyon road. In 6/10ths of a mile, there will be a well-defined scrambleway on the left. Take this down to the canyon bottom. Once in the canyon, turn upstream and boulder-hop up the canyon for about 1/10th of a mile to reach the better climbing sites.

If coming from the Pacific Coast Highway, park just before a "NO PARKING" sign identical to the one described above. Again, be very cautious while hiking up the busy road. In about 3/4ths mile there will be a paved turnout on the right (it's blocked by a locked gate). From this turnout, either take a *very steep* scrambleway down to the canyon bottom, or walk another 1/10th mile uphill to reach the better path described above.

10

DEVIL'S PUNCHBOWL

DEVIL'S PUNCHBOWL is a superb lead-climbing site which is easily accessible as a day's outing from the Los Angeles area. The "punchbowl" derives its name from the huge cup-shaped sandstone slabs which jut up at near vertical angles, thereby creating some of the most spectacular geologic formations in Southern California. The largest such formation is the main climbing site; it towers several hundred feet above a seasonal stream. Most of the climbs are multipitch, and a few run over 300 feet in length.

Though there are many climbs of only moderate difficulty, DEVIL'S PUNCHBOWL is not recommended for inexperienced climbers. This is because all routes have to be lead, and protection is sometimes questionable. Most of the routes are bolted; however, some bolts are loose and many others are missing hangars. Since new bolting is not allowed, the opportunity to improve protection does not exist.

DEVIL'S PUNCHBOWL is classified by Los Angeles County as a "Natural Area" Park. In such parks, one of the primary objectives is the preservation of natural features. It just so happens that at DEVIL'S PUNCHBOWL the primary attraction of the site (and thus that which rangers most desire to preserve in a natural state) are the huge sandstone slabs: in other words, the climbing walls. In this regard, rangers are adamant about not allowing any new bolting.

(continued on page 62)

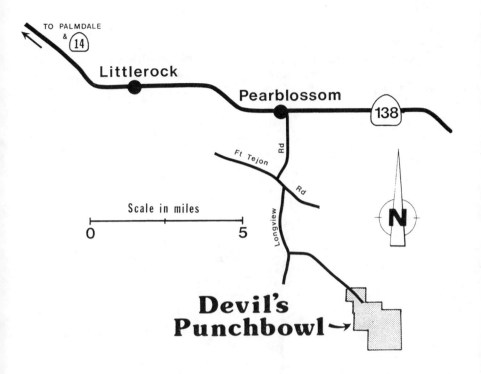

DIRECTIONS

From the Los Angeles area, take Interstate 14 north towards Palmdale. Exit 14 onto the Pearblossom Highway, which is a few miles south of Palmdale. Continue on the Pearblossom Highway (following signs to Littlerock) until its intersection with Route 138 (about 5½ miles). Turn right onto 138 (again, following signs to Littlerock). Alternatively, 138 can be reached directly from Palmdale — take the "Palmdale Boulevard" offramp and head east.

The turnoff to Devil's Punchbowl is at the east edge of the little town of Pearblossom, about four miles past Littlerock. At Pearblossom, turn right onto Longview Road; this turn is marked by a sign indicating directions to Devil's Punchbowl. In slightly over one mile, turn left onto Fort Tejon Road, then make an immediate right back onto Longview. From this intersection, follow signs to the Punchbowl (it's another 5½ miles up the hill).

Furthermore, the use of chalk is discouraged as it tends to leave long-lasting visual scars (there is a general lack of rain in the area). Finally, large groups or climbing organizations typically are not allowed to climb in the park.

As a final note, it should be mentioned that the Punchbowl can be quite hot in Summer, and snow is possible in Winter. The best climbing seasons are thus Spring and Fall.

CLIMBING NOTES

Twenty-one routes are presented here; all but four lie on the main climbing formation, which is known as the V.D. (Very Direct) Wall. The remaining four are on Wallbanger Wall, which is located immediately behind the V.D. Wall. To reach these sites, take the Burkhart Loop Trail from the south side of the parking area (be careful not to confuse the loop trail with the Burkhart Horse Trail). A short and easy downhill hike along the loop trail leads to the climbing sites. To reach the base of the V.D. Wall, leave the main trail at the point where there is a wire guardrail and follow various scrambleways to the canyon bottom.

Most routes are protected by bolts, but many are without hangars. It's thus helpful to bring along some small wired stoppers which can be cinched over hangarless bolts. In addition to the wired stoppers, a selection of Friends is quite useful. Most cracks are shallow and/or bottoming — thus the need for Friends.

Though it is possible to walk off many of the routes, descent is frequently by rappel. One rope is usually sufficient; however, two full-length ropes are required to reach the ground from the popular rappel site above the UPPER BOLT ROUTE.

CLIMBING ROUTES: V.D. WALL

If the above directions are followed to V.D. Wall, you will enter the streambed almost directly in front of the WATER CRACKS (route #6). Routes 1 & 2 are then downstream to your left, Routes 3 — 8 are in the immediate vicinity, and Routes 9 — 21 are upstream to your right.

1.   **JULIETTE'S FLAKE, LEFT**   5.6   (Not pictured)

JULIETTE'S FLAKE is the obvious 75 ft. high flake on the eastern edge of V.D. Wall; it's about 100 yards left of the WATER CRACKS Route. Climb the chimney on the flake's left side — large hexes provide the best protection. Descent is by rappel; one rope suffices.

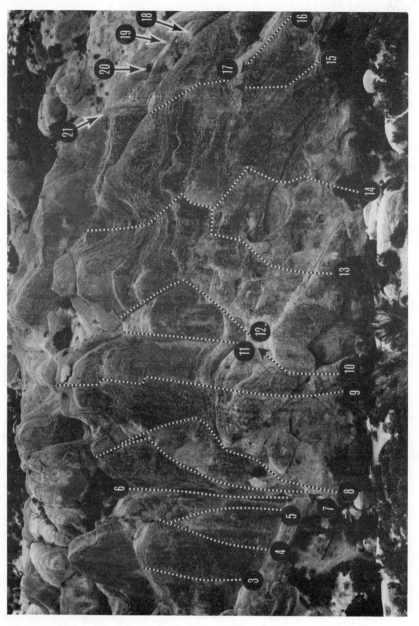

MAIN CLIMBING AREA - Devil's Punchbowl

2.   JULIETTE'S FLAKE, RIGHT   5.7   (Not Pictured)

Ascend the layback crack on the right side of JULIETTE'S FLAKE (see description for route #1).

3.   TENACIOUS   5.10

There are three excellent climbs on the face immediately to the left of the WATER CRACKS (route #6). TENACIOUS follows the left-most line of bolts.

4.   VELCRO   5.9

This is the middle line of bolts on the face just left of the WATER CRACKS. Start a few feet left of an obvious white streak and follow the bolts up and right to the top of the streak.

5.   RURP RIP-OFF   5.9

Follow the line of bolts to the right of the white streak described in route #4, ending at same point as route #4.

6.   WATER CRACKS   5.8

Follow obvious crack system to a belay anchor in the large alcove above. A second pitch of combined chimney/crack leads to the top.

7.   SLOT MACHINE   5.8

Follow the obvious layback crack which starts from the same alcove as WATER CRACKS. Angle up and right to reach a left-leaning jamcrack which heads to the summit. Three pitches.

8.　TREE CORNER　　　　　　　5.8

Follow crack and chimney on left edge of main face to reach a pine tree above. From the tree, angle up and right to reach a left-facing groove. Follow this groove to reach the left-leaning jamcrack of SLOT MACHINE. Three pitches.

9.　LOWER BOLT ROUTE　　　　　5.10+

Follow the line of bolts (many of which are hangarless) about 30 feet left of a landmark horseshoe-shaped overhang. Follow bolts past two overhangs to reach a hanging belay site. Continue to an overhanging flake, which is passed on the left. A short steep wall leads to the top. Three pitches.

10.　OVERHANGER　　　　　　　5.9

Ascend the left side of the horseshoe-shaped overhang to reach the steep face above. Continue in the crack which diagonals up and right to reach the start of the UPPER BOLT ROUTE. Can be lead or top-roped. For top-roping, walk up the ramp (see route #11) to reach an obvious belay anchor.

11.　UPPER BOLT ROUTE　　　　　5.6

Walk up the obvious ramp which starts to the right of the landmark Horseshoe Overhang, and set up a belay immediately above this overhang. Two pitches follow the obvious groove above. It's possible to walk off the backside; however, the UPPER BOLT ROUTE is a popular rappel site. Two full-length ropes are required to reach the ground.

12.　DIAGONAL LEFT　　　　　　5.6

From the start of route #11, easy climbing angles up and right to reach a left-leaning crack. Follow this back to the top of route #11. Medium to large chocks and/or Friends are required. Two pitches.

13. FOLLOWER'S FOLLY 5.9

Climb the face below the ramp (see route #11), beginning at a point about 25 feet left of the ramp's start. Climb past a bolt to reach the ramp, then ascend ramp a few feet. Climb face above into a depression, then angle right to a belay above a block. From this block, climb the face above till it's possible to traverse right to a chimney/flake. Climb this flake to reach second belay site above. Finish via the large groove to the left, or traverse far left to the top of the UPPER BOLT ROUTE. Three pitches.

14. REQUIEM 5.10+

Start on the face about ten feet right of the landmark ramp. Follow bolts as route zig-zags back and forth to reach a hole-in-the-rock "arch." From this "arch," angle up and left to pick up FOLLOWER'S FOLLY at the short chimney/flake. Three pitches.

15. REVERSE TRAVERSE 5.9

Start on a pedestal, which is 30 — 40 feet left of the V.D. Wall's western edge. Ascend a ramp up and left to a bolt, then angle up and right to the first belay anchor on CHALICE. Continue on LEADER'S FRIGHT, traverse left on CHALICE, or rappel off.

16. CHALICE 5.4

Start about 15 — 20 feet left of the V.D. Wall's western edge. Climb straight up past a bolt, turn the corner, and work across ledges to the first anchor. Either rappel off, or continue traversing left to the second belay anchor on FOLLOWER'S FOLLY. From this anchor, the route traverses still further left to end at the top anchor of the UPPER BOLT ROUTE. These long traverses are protected by bolts.

17. LEADER'S FRIGHT   5.6

From the first anchor on CHALICE, climb up to the ridge top. The route angles up and left after the first depression is reached. The anchor on top is not recommended for rappelling as the numerous ledges are likely to cause rope damage.

WALLBANGER WALL

Wallbanger Wall is located immediately behind V.D. Wall. To reach it, turn the western corner of V.D. Wall and scramble over rocks a short ways up the streambed. Take the first canyon on the left — Wallbanger Wall forms the right-hand side of this little canyon.

Routes 18 & 20 are best top-roped — ascend PHILIP'S CRACK to set up the top-rope belay. The descent for all routes is by rappel from the anchor located immediately above THE MOON.

18. SIDESWIPE   5.5

Top-rope climb; ascend the face two feet right of PHILIP'S CRACK.

19. PHILIP'S CRACK   5.2

Ascend the obvious crack which is located a short ways up the canyon (on the right-hand side).

20. THE MOON   5.8 - 5.9

Top-rope climb; ascend the face about fifteen feet left of PHILIP'S CRACK. Climb to obvious hole; four variations are possible above — all are 5.8 - 5.9.

21. HARVEY WALLBANGER   5.4
Ascend the obvious crack in a corner, which is about 100 yards up the canyon from the streambed. A 4th class descent is required to reach the rappel anchor above THE MOON.

*Matt Oliphant leading the
LOWER BOLT ROUTE.*

11

PACIFICO

PACIFICO is one of three popular climbing sites (the other two being Horse Flats and Williamson Rock) in the San Gabriel Mountains, which form the northern perimeter of the Los Angeles basin. Since 95% of the San Gabriels lie within Angeles National Forest, the mountainous environs are commonly referred to by the term "Angeles."

The three Angeles Crest climbing sites are only about an hour's drive above La Cañada and thus are reasonably accessible to anyone living in the San Fernando Valley or northern Los Angeles areas. On the other hand, none of the three warrant a longer drive — at least not when considered individually. In this respect, climbing along the Angeles Crest is rather reminiscent of the Big Bear/Running Springs area. In both cases, there is sufficient climbing to justify a longer drive if all the sites are combined into an overnight outing.

PACIFICO is the authors' choice for the best of the three Angeles Crest sites. It's possible to drive right up to the climbing formation, there are climbs suitable for both leading and top-roping, and there are routes for climbers of all experience levels. The rock is good quality granite, and though the routes tend to be short, there are several that are almost one full pitch. The mountain offers magnificent panoramic views, and at an elevation of almost 7,000 feet, PACIFICO is the highest and thus the coolest of the three San Gabriel sites. Finally, there's a good campground only about a mile away.

DIRECTIONS

In La Cañada (just east of Pasadena), exit the 210 Freeway onto the Angeles Crest Highway (Route 2). Head north into the mountains and follow the winding Route 2 for approximately 25 miles. A good landmark to look for is Newcomb's Ranch Restaurant. Two miles past Newcomb's, turn left onto Santa Clara Divide Road. Follow this road four miles (driving past Horse Flats campground), and turn left onto a dirt road marked by a sign indicating directions to Pacifico campground. In 4.2 miles there will be a wide turnout with an unmarked dirt road to the right. Take this unmarked road — it leads to Pacifico campground. The turnoff to the climbing formation will appear on the left in about 1/2 mile (this turnoff is marked by a sign for the Pacific Crest Trail). From the PCT sign, follow the rough dirt road west about 3/4 mile to the climbing site. This road is barely passable by two-wheel drive vehicles; it's in such poor shape that it's recommended primarily for 4-wheel drive vehicles. Others may wish to park and hike in the last half mile or so.

71

CLIMBING ROUTES

1. **CRACK/FACE**   5.9

    Two of the best routes are located on the lower section of
    PACIFICO'S east face. Look for a comparatively smooth wall
    that is split by a series of cracks which run from upper left to
    lower right. This route starts in a shallow trough immediately
    left of the smooth face. Follow the thin crack till it's possible
    to transfer to the face, bypassing the bulge on its right side.
    Proceed straight up after the bulge is passed.

2. **CRACK/FACE**   5.11

    This route goes up the wall described above. Start in the
    lower right-hand corner, and climb past a bolt and fixed pin.
    At the second fixed pin (unusable), stand in the sloping pocket
    to reach a second bolt up and left. Easier climbing continues
    to lead up and left.

3. **CRACK**   5.10

    Look for a shallow right-facing open book that's tucked behind
    a tree a few feet to the right of route #2. Lieback the finger
    crack found in this corner, and then follow the double crack
    system above. Recommended for top-roping.

4. **FACE**   5.10

    Ascend the smooth face immediately to the right of route #2,
    finishing by way of the double crack system above. Recommended for top-roping.

(Routes continued on page 74)

Pacifico, Main Wall

A. *Upper Wall (See page 74)*   B. *West Wall (See Page 75)*

73

5. **CRACK** 5.5

On the northeast corner (to the right of routes 3 & 4), there are two long right-leaning cracks. The left crack is an awkward off-width.

6. **CRACK** 5.3

Ascend the crack about five feet to the right of route #5. This crack is much easier and cleaner.

MISCELLANEOUS CLIMBING

A. **UPPER WALL** (See photo on previous page)

A short upper climbing wall can be reached by scrambling over broken rocks at PACIFICO'S southeast corner (to the left of routes 1 & 2 described on the previous pages). Two good routes can be found here:

1. **CRACK/FACE** 5.9

Climb straight up the obvious crack on the left side of the upper wall. This starts as a face climb, then turns into an awkward off-width.

2. **FACE** 5.6

Climb the face, following a hairline crack about six feet to the right of route #1 above. This climb is further identified by a hangarless bolt found about halfway up.

Karin Spithorst on the West Face Crack

B.   WEST FACE

Additional climbing can be found on PACIFICO'S back side (i.e., the west side). This west face is a slightly overhanging formation that offers good opportunities for aid practice and/or some extremely difficult free climbing. One of the best routes is the crack about fifteen feet down from the wall's left edge. There are good holds, but the climbing is strenuous (5.7).

*Matt Dancy bouldering near the main
climbing area, Mount Pacifico.*

BOULDERING

Good bouldering can be found throughout the Mount Pacifico area. Many problems can be found in the immediate vicinity of the main climbing formation (see photo above). Elsewhere, there are numerous bouldering sites along the dirt road which leads to Pacifico campground, and the campground itself has some particularly good possibilities.

12

HORSEFLATS

HORSE FLATS has a respectable climbing wall; however, it's small and hard to find. Those who are energetic enough to seek it out will find some great climbing, most of which is quite difficult. Of the seven routes described in the next pages, five are 5.10+ or harder. The climbing wall is thus recommended primarily for serious and experienced climbers.

On the other hand, HORSE FLATS has excellent bouldering that can be enjoyed by everyone. The boulders are of high quality granite, and there are lots of them. And — in contrast to the climbing wall — they are readily accessible. Specific information on bouldering problems has not been included here. HORSE FLATS has yet to be heavily developed, and newcomers can still find and develop their own original routes.

See page 82 for directions to the bouldering area. To reach the climbing wall, park at the twin water tanks found near the campground entrance. Hike up the prominent gully directly opposite the water tanks. Start by following the path on the left-hand side, then after about 1/2 mile cross over to the right. From this point, the climbing site will be a little further uphill and to the right. The site looks like a jumble of rocks — distinguishable from many others only in that it's larger. Allow about 15 - 20 minutes for the hike in.

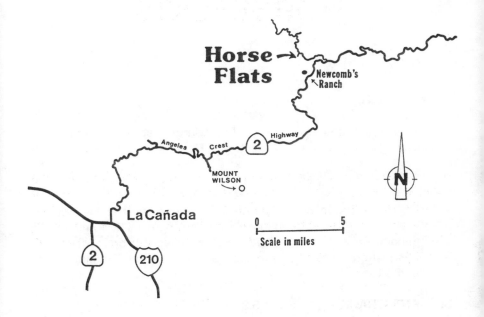

DIRECTIONS

In La Cañada (just east of Pasadena), exit the 210 Freeway onto the Angeles Crest Highway (Route 2). Head north into the mountains and follow the winding Route 2 for approximately 25 miles. A good landmark to look for is Newcomb's Ranch Restaurant. Two miles past Newcomb's, turn left onto Santa Clara Divide Road and follow the signs to Horse Flats Campground. The campground host may request that you pay to park inside the campground, in which case it might be reasonable to park outside and walk in.

CLIMBING ROUTES

1. **CORNER**   **5.11+**

   Follow the double crack on the corner just left of Route #2.
   Traverse right under the roof to join Route #2.

2. **ANT LINE**   **5.11+**

   On the left side of the climbing formation, start in the shallow
   corner dihedral and follow it up and right as it turns into a
   lieback flake. Traverse right across a very prominent undercling, then transfer to the face above. Easier climbing leads
   to the top.

3. **ANT CRACK**   **5.8**

   Head straight up the crack immediately right of Route #2.

4. **BLACK STREAK, LEFT** **5.10+**

   There are two black streaks on a knobby face to the right of
   the chimney which splits the main climbing formation. This
   route goes up the face between the two streaks.

5. **BLACK STREAK, RIGHT** **5.10+**

   Climb the face to the right of the right-hand black streak (see
   description of Route #4 above).

Horse Flats

6. BREAK FOR DAYLIGHT 5.7 (Not pictured)

A very large split rock leans against the right-hand edge of the main climbing formation, thereby forming a narrow cave. About 15 feet into the cave, there is a narrow crack on the left wall.   This can be climbed as a crack (5.7) or as a chimney by making use of the right wall (easy 5th class).

7. BAT FLAKE ARETE   5.11+ (Not pictured)

There's a smooth overhanging face on the right side of the leaning rock described in Route #6 above. Ascend the notched corner to the left of this face, exiting onto knobby holds high and left.

81

Mike Ayon on BAT FLAKE ARETE

BOULDERING

As mentioned at the start of this section, HORSE FLATS has superb bouldering potential. Climbable rock can be found most anywhere, but the best concentration of decent boulders is found at the southwest corner of the campground. To reach this bouldering area, hike up the trail that starts in the SW corner (opposite campsite #7). It's only about a five minute walk to the first good boulders. Initially the better boulders are to the left of the trail, but they begin to appear on both sides as one hikes further uphill.

*Roger Whitehead bouldering at
Horse Flats Campground*

13

WILLIAMSON ROCK

WILLIAMSON ROCK is not only the largest of the three Angeles Crest sites, it is also one of the best sport crags in Southern California. It's situated at an elevation of about 7,000 feet, and offers delightful climbing in a subalpine setting. The area receives heavy snow in the winter, but climbing is possible during the other three seasons.

When this book was first published in 1988, WILLIAMSON ROCK was not highly-developed. The authors discussed the rock's virtues, and issued a call for climbers to develop the site. Perhaps climbers answered the call, or perhaps it was just coincidence, but the area has received heavy attention since 1989. There were just a handful of known routes in 1988; today there are more than a hundred. Troy Mayr has written an excellent guide to the area (*Sport Crags in Southern California*), and his book should be consulted for route information.

Multi-pitch climbs of up to 300 feet have been established. There is some loose rock, but most routes are on solid granite. There are a lot of well-protected sport routes, and many top-roping opportunities also exist.

The original route descriptions from the 1988 edition are included in the following pages; this information is still useful for someone taking a first, exploratory trip to the site.

Unfortunately, a bit of a hike is required to reach the rock. There are two trails which can be found at the northeast corner of the parking turnout. Take the one which heads downhill and back to the west. This trail crosses a stream (where there are several large cement pipes), angles south from there, then abruptly cuts back to the north. Just past this point, look for scrambleways on the left which drop into the canyon below. Once in the canyon, follow the stream downhill to the climbing area. The base of the lower wall is marked by a cool and shady grove of cedar and a large prominent boulder. The upper climbing area is reached by a long scramble up the canyon around the corner to the right.

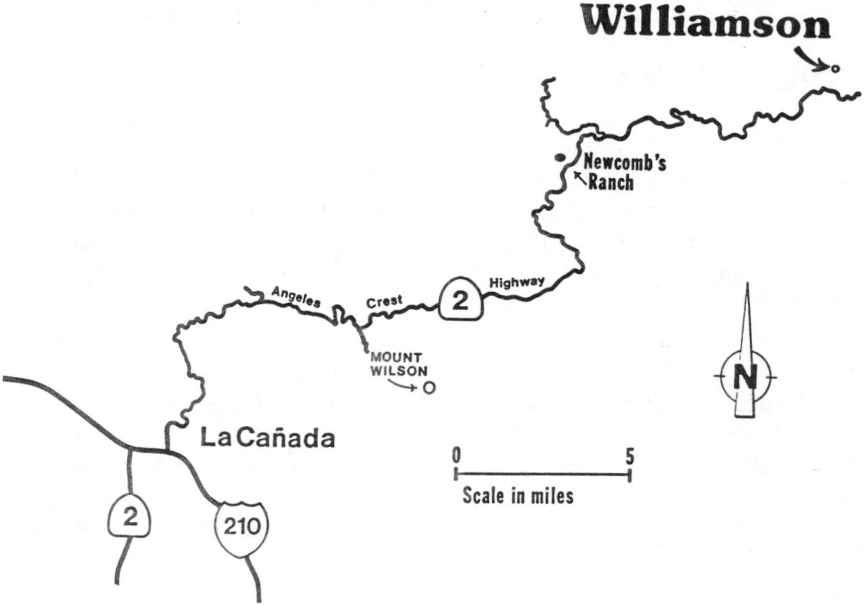

Williamson

Newcomb's
Ranch

Angeles Crest **2** Highway

MOUNT
WILSON
→ O

La Cañada

N

0   5
Scale in miles

2   210

DIRECTIONS

In La Cañada (just east of Pasadena), exit the 210 Freeway onto the Angeles Crest Highway (Route 2). Head north into the mountains and follow the winding Route 2 for approximately 35 miles, driving past both the Mount Waterman and Kratka Ridge ski areas. A good landmark to look for is Eagles Roost Picnic Area, which appears on the right about 1½ miles past Kratka Ridge. Parking for WILLIAMSON ROCK is the large turnout on the left about 3/4ths mile beyond Eagles Roost.

CLIMBING ROUTES

UPPER CLIMBING AREA

1. FACE   5.7

Climb the shallow trough located about 50 feet left of the more obvious waterchute of Route #2. The crux is the bulge; easier climbing above leads to the top.

2. WATERCHUTE   5.9

There are two prominent waterchutes on the upper wall; this route goes up the left chute. Again, the crux is the bulge near the beginning. There are two belay bolts at the top for protection.

LOWER CLIMBING AREA

3. FACE   5.9

Start in the easy trough at the left edge of the lower wall. Follow this as it angles up and right to a pocket. From the pocket, difficult and poorly-protected climbing surmounts the bulge above.

4. FACE/CHIMNEY   5.6

Start in the trough of Route #3, but at the pocket traverse right to the chimney of Route #5.

5. FACE/CHIMNEY   5.5

Follow the line of bolts adjacent to a left-facing and left-leaning open book (on the right side of the lower wall). Exit via the chimney above.

Williamson Rock

14

DEEP CREEK NARROWS

Running Springs' DEEP CREEK NARROWS —as its name implies — is a climbing site located deep in a narrow canyon. The climbing opportunities are somewhat limited, and only four routes are described here. But don't let the shortage of routes keep you from visiting this site. The setting is idyllic: the canyon is cool and shady, the rock is imposing, and the year-round stream adds to the overall tranquility. And if that is not enough, the climbing routes themselves are of very high quality. All-in-all, an enjoyable afternoon can be spent at the Narrows.

It is quite understandable that the average climber would not want to drive several hours just to visit the Narrows. There are, however, two other noteworthy climbing sites (Keller Peak & Castle Rock) in the Running Springs/Big Bear area. Taken altogether, these three sites *are* worth the trip — especially if one were to make this a weekend outing.

Park at the point where the dirt road forks (see map & directions). Take the bridle trail to the left of the parking area, being careful not to confuse the left-hand road fork with the bridle trail. Follow the trail downhill approximately 1/4 mile to a fenced enclosure. Pick up a new trail (dirt road) on the far side of this fenced area. Follow the new trail downhill till the top of the climbing site can be seen below; from this point, an easy scramble leads to the canyon bottom. The trail forks several times, and the approach can be a little confusing. Just keep in mind that you want to head downhill to the canyon bottom, and you will eventually find the rock.

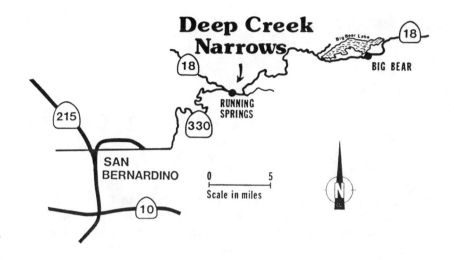

DIRECTIONS

From the city of San Bernardino, exit 215 onto 30 East (marked "Highland Avenue/Mountain Resorts"). At freeway's end, turn left onto Highland Avenue. Continue east on Highland as it becomes Highway 330, and follow this to Running Springs. In Running Springs, 330 joins 18; turn right onto 18.

From the intersection of 330 & 18, go approximately 2/10ths of a mile and turn left onto Hunsaker Way. Take the first left (West Drive). Follow West Drive to Cove Circle and turn right. At the crest of the hill is an intersection with a dirt road — turn left and follow the dirt road to a stop sign. Park here. See previous page for walking directions to climbing site.

CLIMBING ROUTES

1. **CRACK**   **5.7**

   Approach by down-climbing from the left top. Follow obvious crack.

2. **CORNER**   **5.9**

   Approach by down-climbing over blocks from the top of route #3. Stem & Bridge to a small sloping ledge, then transfer to face on the left. The crux involves a strenuous and awkward surmounting of the block above. This is done by a combination layback/jam/mantle.

3. **FACE/CRACK**   **5.7**

   Start in obvious dihedral at the left corner of the Narrows' main face. Follow crack up and right. There are good holds throughout, and this is an enjoyable and highly recommended climb.

4. **FACE**   **5.10**

   Proceed straight up the right-hand corner, making use of holds on the face to the left.

DEEP CREEK NARROWS

15

KELLER PEAK

Like WILLIAMSON ROCK, KELLER PEAK has been highly developed since the original 1988 edition of this book was published. It is now a premier sport crag with over twenty routes, many of which are well-protected sport climbs. There are only three routes easier than 5.10, thus this area primarily attracts experienced climbers. It's a good place to push limits, and/or get a superb workout.

KELLER PEAK is a small crag, but this disadvantage is offset by many attractions. In addition to the quality of the climbing, the pristine mountain setting and ease of access are big inducements to visit the site. Also, there is ample opportunity for bouldering in the immediate vicinity. The area is usually closed in the winter, but open during the spring, summer, and fall. In the summer, climbing is best enjoyed in the morning or evening, as KELLER PEAK tends to get rather hot.

Good campsites can be found along Keller Peak Road. Bring plenty of water; none is available at the campground.

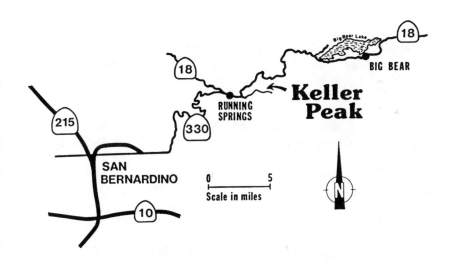

DIRECTIONS

From the city of San Bernardino, exit 215 onto 30 East (marked "Highland Avenue/Mountain Resorts"). At freeway's end, turn left onto Highland Avenue. Continue east on Highland as it becomes Highway 30, and follow this to Running Springs. In Running Springs, 330 joins 18 — turn right onto 18.

From the intersection of 330 & 18, go east on Highway 18 approximately one mile and turn onto Keller Peak Road. The climbing site is on the left 3.5 miles up this road. Parking is limited; however, there is space for one or two vehicles on the side of the road adjacent to the climbing area.

CLIMBING ROUTES

1. **MORE PUNK THAN FUNK**   5.10+
    Follow the obvious crack about fifteen feet left of route #2.
    Bolted routes to immediate left (EVE OF THE RING and
    ORANGE TAPESTRY respectively) are both 5.12+.

2. **MORE MOSS THAN GLOSS**   5.9
    Climb knobs and crack to notch above.

3. **CRACK**   5.8
    Climb the crack about five feet to the left of a squeeze
    chimney (the chimney itself is a 5.9 route).

4. **GRAVITATIONAL HUMILIATION** 5.11+
    Follow bolt line on face immediately to right of Route #3.

5. **BOILERMAKER**   5.10+
    Ascend the awkward-looking crack which is about ten feet to
    the left of a large and obvious flake.

6. **EASY CRACK**   5.8
    Ascend the weathered crack just left of the rock's uphill edge.
    There are good holds, but the climb is strenuous and awkward.

7. **ARETE**   5.10
    Top-rope climb just right of route #6.

NOTE: For additional route information, refer to Troy Mayr's *Sport
Crags in Southern California.*

KELLER PEAK

CASTLE ROCK

Big Bear Lake as seen from the summit of Castle Rock.

THE CASTLE ROCK described here is a Southern California climbing site. This can be a little confusing since there's another climbing locality of the same name in the Bay area. The fact that the other Castle Rock is better known should not deter anyone from visiting this one. It is — stated quite simply — the best of the three Running Springs/Big Bear sites.

Big Bear's CASTLE ROCK is appropriately named; the climbing formation has buttresses which jut up over 100 feet in height. Though the climbing opportunities are somewhat limited, there are nonetheless some routes of very high quality. Also, a good part of CASTLE ROCK'S appeal is found in its tranquil setting. It's on a cool and shady hillside above Big Bear Lake, and the summit affords an impressive panoramic view of the lake. All things considered, Big Bear's CASTLE ROCK is deserving of greater recognition by Southern California climbers.

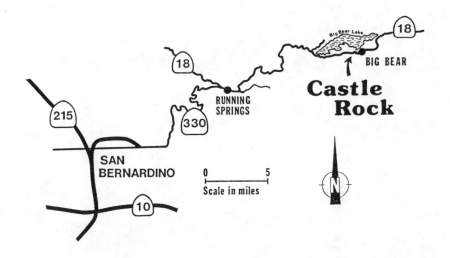

DIRECTIONS

From the city of San Bernardino, exit 215 onto 30 East (marked "Highland Avenue/Mountain Resorts"). At freeway's end, turn left onto Highland Avenue. Continue east on Highland as it becomes Highway 330, and follow this to Running Springs. In Running Springs, 330 joins 18; turn right onto 18.

From the junction of 330 and 18, head east on 18 towards the town of Big Bear. Continue following 18 as it crosses the dam, and look for the trailhead on the right 1/10th mile before reaching the Big Bear city limits. There is a turnout for parking on the left.

From the parking area, hike the maintained trail to Castle Rock, which is about one mile above the road. The path climbs to a small crest, where there is a trail intersection. Follow the trail to the left (marked "Castle Rock"); this leads to the right-hand base of the climbing formation. CAUTION: Rattlesnakes have been spotted along these trails.

OVERVIEW OF CASTLE ROCK, AS SEEN FROM THE EAST. LETTERED ARROWS DENOTE ROUTE-FINDING LANDMARKS.

A.   Southeast Corner (Routes 1 & 2)

B.   Chimney (Route 3)

C.   Smooth Face (Not visible in photo) (Route 4)

D.   Area of Routes 5 - 9

Chris Hsu Climbing the 5.10 Crack (Route #4)

CLIMBING ROUTES

1. **CRACK**   5.6

   There is a hand crack six feet to the left of the chock stone of route #2. Climb up this crack using good holds on the face to reach an eight-foot column. Undercling the left-angling crack above.

2. **CRACK**   5.8

   At the S.E. corner (to the right of two Jeffrey pines growing at the bottom of an obvious prow), there is a fat & squat chock stone. Enter the crack at the top right side of this chock stone, and continue up the zigzag—bearing slightly right where the zipper-like crack opens out to boulders above.

3. **CHIMNEY**   5.9

   There is a large chimney around the corner to the right of route #2. Climb the chimney until forced to transfer to the face to the left, and then follow the crack above.

4. **CRACK**   5.10

   There is a blank face with a bolt ladder 20 feet to the right of route #3. Climb the crack to the left of this face and continue to the prominent crack above.

Castle Rock, Left

5.   FACE   5.4

There is a large boulder leaning against the wall about six feet left of the chimney (see route #6). Climb the wall to the right of this boulder making use of wide cracks and prominent holds. Continue up the wall to the right of a finger column while making your way to the horn above.

6.   CHIMNEY   5.7

This route follows a deep chimney which is obstructed by a large chock stone twelve feet up. Climb up and over the chock stone, then continue by making use of the prominent deep crack on the left side of a narrow column.

7.   CRACK/FACE   5.9   (Variation 5.6)

There is a crack formed by a column fifteen feet right of route #6. This column is wider at the top than at the bottom, and the crack flares open halfway up. Climb this crack to the top of the column, then bear slightly left and climb the broken face above. For an easier variation   (5.6), bypass the difficult face by traversing right from the top of the column and exiting at the triangular chock stone (see route #8).

8.   CRACK   5.7

Ascend the deep crack immediately to the right of route #7, and exit at the prominent triangular chock stone above.

9.   OFF-WIDTH   5.8

At the north end of the climbing wall, there is a prow with a smooth face which forms a left-facing open book where it meets a large square block. The route starts with the off-width crack in the corner of this book, then continues up and left over jumbled rocks. Exit at the triangular chock stone of route #8.

Castle Rock, Right

17

JOSHUA TREE

JOSHUA TREE hardly needs an introduction. Not only is it one of the two best Southern California sites, it also enjoys an international reputation. When other California sites such as TAHQUITZ and YOSEMITE are bathed in cold and snow, JOSHUA TREE is typically aglow with warm winter sunshine. Thus climbers flock to this desert area — not only from Southern California, but also from around the world.

Clement weather is by no means JOSHUA TREE's only attraction. Indeed, the area's primary draw is the quantity and quality of the climbing. Joshua Tree National Monument covers half a million acres, the western half of which abounds with climbable crags and outcroppings. More than 1,400 routes have been recorded; these range from twenty to several hundred feet in length. Many can be top-roped; however, most are typically lead.

The rock is quartz monzonite, which is a crystalline form of granite. The crystalline nature of the rock provides both good and bad conditions for climbers. On the good side, its roughness allows for better friction on face climbs and more secure holds in the numerous jam cracks and chimneys. But on the bad side, the rock is merciless on a climber's hands.

Numerous guidebooks cover the climbing at JOSHUA TREE. The two most prominent are *Joshua Tree Climber's Guide* by Randy Vogel and *A Climber's Guide to Joshua Tree National Monument* by John Wolfe and Bob Dominick. Because climbing information is covered in depth by these other books, the presentation that follows is quite limited in scope — the intent here is merely to introduce JOSHUA TREE to the first-time visitor.

Though the monument has dozens of highly developed sites, the climbing in and around Hidden Valley Campground is generally acknowledged to be among the best. Accordingly, it is this area which is covered here. Sufficient route information is provided to fill an initial weekend or two. But it should be noted that this coverage of Hidden Valley is not intended to be complete. Anyone desiring more detailed information on Hidden Valley Campground (and on the rest of the monument) should consult the books mentioned above.

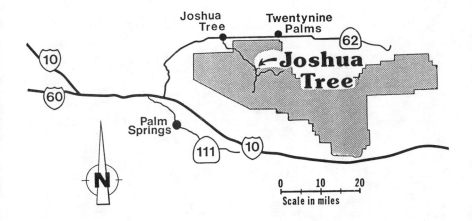

DIRECTIONS

The most frequently used approach to Joshua Tree is via Interstate 10.   Exit I-10 on Highway 62, about five miles east of the turnoff to Palm Springs.   Follow 62 about 28 miles to the town of Joshua Tree, and there look for the well-marked turnoff to the National Monument. Hidden Valley Campground is on the left, about 10 miles into Joshua Tree National Monument.

NOTE: A fee is required to enter the monument.

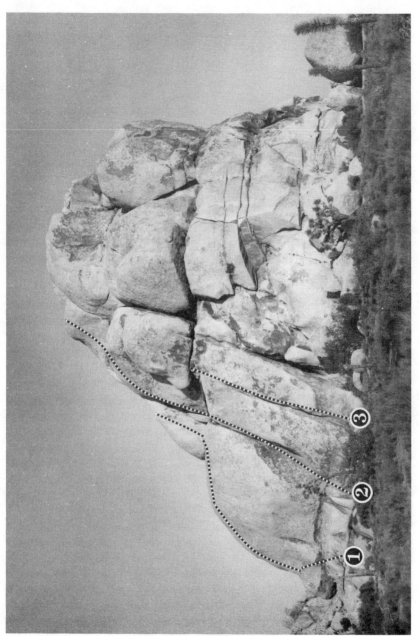

Intersection Rock - South Face

INTERSECTION ROCK

INTERSECTION ROCK is the large dome just across the road from the entrance to Hidden Valley Campground. There are rappel bolts on top.

CLIMBING ROUTES:
INTERSECTION ROCK, SOUTH FACE

1. **BONGLEDESCH**   5.10c

Mantle onto face to the left of an obvious cleft, traverse left, then follow bolts to the large ledge above. Continue up buttress a few feet to the left of the second pitch of Mike's Books (see Route #2).

2. **MIKE'S BOOKS**   5.6 (5.8)

Ascend the prominent dihedral to the large ledge above. The difficult direct start (5.8) can be avoided by traversing to the dihedral from the left (5.6). The second pitch ascends a smaller dihedral above an obvious triangular block. Finish via the face above.

3. **THE WATERCHUTE**   5.9

Ascend the obvious chute to the right of Mike's Books (Route #2). The opening move is the crux.

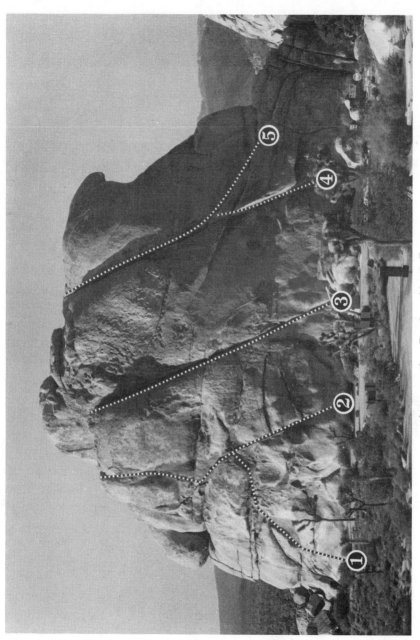

Intersection Rock – North Face

CLIMBING ROUTES:
INTERSECTION ROCK, NORTH FACE

1. **ZIGZAG**   **5.7**

    Easy friction face climbing leads up and right to a ledge, which
    is followed to Half Track (Route #2). Ascend the top portion
    of Half Track to reach the obvious chimney above.

2. **HALF TRACK**   **5.10A**

    Ascend the left-most of three parallel cracks.

3. **LEFT SKI TRACK**   **5.11A**

    Ascend the center crack.

4. **RIGHT SKI TRACK, LOWER**   **5.10B**

    Ascend difficult left-facing & left-leaning dihedral. Climb past
    prominent overhang to reach Route #5.

5. **RIGHT SKI TRACK, UPPER**   **5.3**

    Scramble up the northwest corner of Intersection Rock to
    reach the upper start of the Right Ski Track.

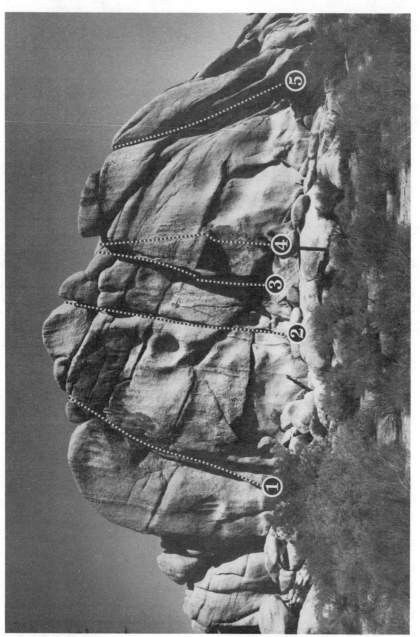

Old Woman — West Face

THE OLD WOMAN

THE OLD WOMAN is the prominent formation in the southwest corner of Hidden Valley Campground. It is further identified by being the first formation on the left as seen entering the campground.

CLIMBING ROUTES:
OLD WOMAN, WEST FACE

1. **DOGLEG**   5.8

   Ascend the curving chimney on the left side of the west face.

2. **DOUBLE CROSS**   5.8

   Jam and lieback the obvious crack near the center of the west face. Highly recommended.

3. **DOUBLE START**   5.7

   Ascend the split chimney about 15 feet to the right of Double Cross (route #2).

4. **BAND SAW**   5.10C

   Ascend the face about 10 feet right of Route #3. Climb past bolt to overhang, then continue up and left.

5. **ORPHAN**   5.9

   Ascend the cleft on the right-hand edge of the west face — it's immediately above a small pinyon pine tree.

Old Woman – East Face

CLIMBING ROUTES:
THE OLD WOMAN, EAST FACE

1. **JUDAS**   5.10B

Ascend overhanging jam crack to face above. Face climb up and right to a hand traverse.

2. **BEARDED CABBAGE**   5.10C

Hand traverse left to reach a vertical crack. Follow right-hand crack, then transfer left to a second crack.

3. **SPIDER LINE**   5.11C

Ascend overhanging crack up corner of a right-leaning & right-facing dihedral. Finish via jam crack above.

4. **DEVIATE**   5.10A

From center of main face, surmount a bulge (protected by a bolt) to reach a second bolt on the face above. Angle up and right to a ledge, then follow chimney to a belay/rappel site. Either rap off or finish via Geronimo (Route #5).

5. **GERONIMO**   5.7

From the belay stance of Deviate (route #4), ascend the split roof up and left. Strenuous.

6. **TABBY LITTER**   5.8

Ascend short jam crack on right edge of face.

The Blob — Northwest Face

THE BLOB

THE BLOB is the large formation north-northwest of The Old Woman. Its northwest face has three short, but enjoyable climbs.

CLIMBING ROUTES:
THE BLOB, NORTHWEST FACE

1.   **BALLBURY**   5.7

Lieback the flake 30 feet left of The Bong.

2.   **THE BONG**   5.4

Ascend the obvious crack in the center of the northwest face.

3.   **HOBLETT**   5.7

Ascend the crack/overhang 30 feet right of The Bong.

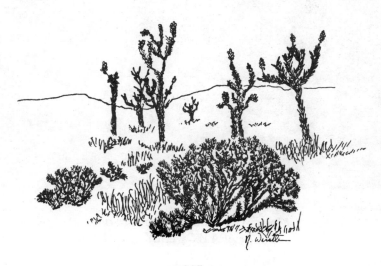

Melanie McNinch on the start of
PAPA WOOLSEY

CLIMBING ROUTES:
THE BLOB, EAST FACE

1. **PAPA WOOLSEY**   **5.10B**
   Ascend the smooth face on the southeast corner of The Blob, climbing past a series of bolts.

2. **MAMA WOOLSEY**   **5.10A**
   Climb the crack/face a few feet right of Papa Woolsey (Route #1). Start in a right-leaning crack to reach mixed face/crack climbing above.

3. **PETE'S HANDFUL**   **5.9**
   Ascend chimney to short jam crack.

4. **SURREALISTIC PILLAR**   **5.10B**
   Ascend crack system on left side of obvious pillar.

117

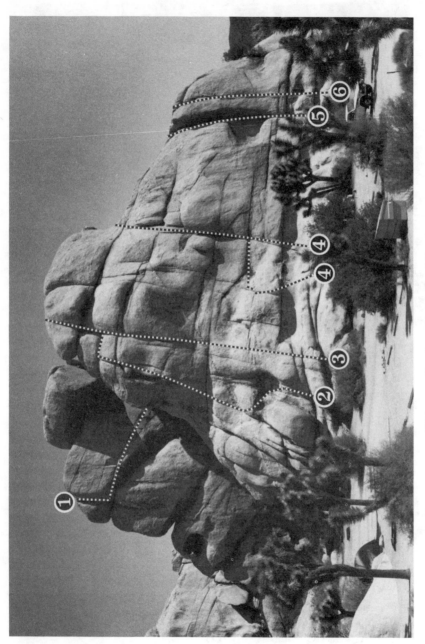

Chimney Rock — Southwest Face

CHIMNEY ROCK

CHIMNEY ROCK is located in the southeast corner of Hidden Valley Campground — it's the first large formation on the right as seen entering the campground.

CLIMING ROUTES:
CHIMNEY ROCK, SOUTHWEST FACE

1. **LOOSE LIPS**   5.11A
Follow horizontal crack left from large chimney, then take off-width to top.

2. **WEST FACE OVERHANG**   5.7
Climb mixed face/crack to reach a squeeze chimney. Above the chimney, follow horizontal crack right to reach a vertical jam crack.

3. **BALLET**   5.10A
Ascend the nearly vertical line of mixed face/crack to reach the top jam crack of route #2.

4. **HOWARD'S HORROR**   5.10B (5.7)
Ascend the crack system near the center of the main face. The 5.7 variation involves an easier start a few feet to the left.

5. **DAMPER**   5.9
Ascend crack in left-facing dihedral.

6. **PINCHED RIB**   5.10A
Climb knobby dike on the face a few feet to the right of Route #5.

Cyclops Rock

CYCLOPS ROCK

Cyclops is the prominent isolated formation about 300 yards east of Hidden Valley Campground. It's readily identified by its single namesake "eye," which is a tunnel through the top center of the main face.

CLIMBING ROUTES: CYCLOPS ROCK

1. **SURFACE TENSION**   5.10C

   Start in an obvious pothole left of the cleft of Route #2. Follow bolts up and left.

2. **THE EYE**   5.3

   Ascend the obvious cleft which leads directly to the namesake "eye." A true classic.

3. **LEADER'S FRIGHT**   5.8

   Climb to large ledge. From right-hand edge of same, follow shallow crack above. This crack is difficult to protect; hence the climb's name.

18

MOUNT RUBIDOUX

MOUNT RUBIDOUX is a boulder-strewn hilltop in the Riverside locality. In addition to the ubiquitous boulders, there are slabs and blocks of all shapes and sizes. The rock is solid quartz monzonite similar to that found at Joshua Tree, and there are some truly classic routes. Some are done as boulder problems, a few others can be lead, but — for the most part — RUBIDOUX is a top-rope site.

Though most of the routes tend to be short, the proliferation of good climbs makes RUBIDOUX an appealing site. Many of the better climbs are on the hill's west side, which almost always gets refreshing breezes. RUBIDOUX can thus be climbed in reasonable comfort year-round.

As might be guessed from the above comments, RUBIDOUX is popular with climbers. It's also popular with hikers, sightseers, bicyclists, and — when the road is open—with motorcyclists and low-riders. Fortunately for climbers, the road is open only for limited hours (Sundays from 9 - 5; Mondays, Tuesdays, and Wednesdays from 10 - 3). When the road *is* open, RUBIDOUX can be quite crowded. If you wish to venture forth on those days, you can drive to the summit from the 7th Street entrance (see map). Otherwise, park at the south entrance and either hike up the road or take the climber's scrambleway to the climbing sites, most of which are near the top.

Steve Mackay has written a guide to RUBIDOUX; unfortunately, it is in limited circulation. If you are lucky enough to obtain a copy, it will lead you to hundreds of climbs. In the meantime, a total of thirty-eight climbs are described here. These include many of the classics, and hopefully you will find them to be a good introduction to MOUNT RUBIDOUX.

As a side note, it should be pointed out that considerable discrepancy exists in regards to the names of climbs at RUBIDOUX. By way of example, the authors have identified *four* different climbs which bear the name "Teflon". Every effort has been made to ensure accuracy; however, you should expect to hear some of the climbs referred to by different names. It can only be hoped that this will not limit anyone's enjoyment of the quality climbing to be found at MOUNT RUBIDOUX.

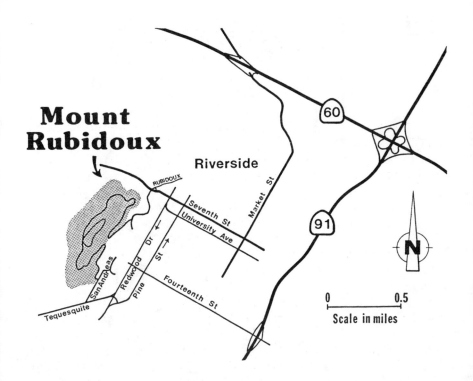

Mount Rubidoux

DIRECTIONS

From Los Angeles:

Head east on Route 60 to Riverside. Exit on Market and head south. Turn right onto 7th Street, go approximately 1/2 mile to Redwood, and turn left. Continue on Redwood to Tequesquite. Turn right onto Tequesquite, then turn right again onto San Andreas. Park opposite the "exit" for the Mount Rubidoux Road.

From Orange County:

Take Route 91 to Riverside and exit at 14th Street. Head west on 14th to Redwood. Turn left onto Redwood, and follow remaining directions as above.

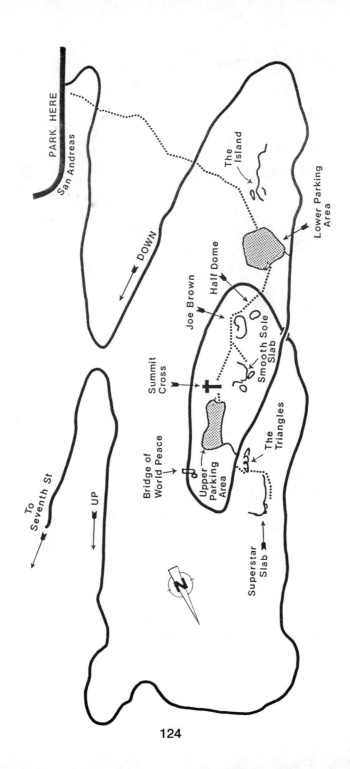

LOCATION OF CLIMBING SITES

A. **SUPERSTAR SLAB:** The Mount Rubidoux road branches at the summit; the left fork ends in the Upper Parking Area, the right fork is the start of the "Down Road" (indicated by a sign painted on a boulder). Step around a pepper tree next to the painted boulder, and descend a steep scrambleway to the base of THE TRIANGLES (site #2, below) From THE TRIANGLES, follow ongoing scrambleways to the north and slightly down. This leads directly to the right-hand edge of SUPERSTAR. Be alert; there's an abundance of poison oak in the SUPERSTAR/ TRIANGLES area.

B. **THE TRIANGLES:** The route to SUPERSTAR SLAB passes the base of THE TRIANGLES. See description above.

C. **ENGLISH SMOOTH SOLE SLAB:** From the summit cross, scramble approximately seventy-five feet due west over various boulders to reach the top of SMOOTH SOLE SLAB. The base is reached by swinging down and to the left.

D. **JOE BROWN BOULDER:** From the summit cross, follow a well-used path southeast along the ridge — this leads to the top of JOE BROWN.

E. **HALF DOME:** This boulder is located slightly west and downhill   from JOE BROWN (see route description above).

F. **THE ISLAND:** This formation is located just south of the Lower Parking Area, and good trails lead directly to the rock.

SUPERSTAR SLAB

SUPERSTAR SLAB is the largest single rock at Mount Rubidoux, and it is the location for some exceptionally fine (but quite difficult) face climbing. It's recommended primarily for the advanced climber.

1. **COATHANGER**   5.12

This climb starts on the face a few feet to the left of Superstar's north prow. Ascend a thin crack to the bolt, traverse right six feet to a chopped bolt, then follow flake around corner to the right.

2. **FROSTY CONE**   5.10+

Start in the small alcove to the right of the north prow. Exit alcove high and left, then follow grey streak to the top.

3. **MONO CONE**   5.10

Ascend short pillar on right-hand edge of alcove (see route #2, above). Mantle onto face, and follow grey streak to the top. Mono Cone parallels Frosty Cone; the former being a few feet to the right of the latter.

4. **SUPERSTAR**   5.9

A large flake leans against the main face of Superstar Slab. From the top of this flake, face climb to ledge above. Easier climbing leads up and right.

5. **FLABOB**   5.11+

To the right of Superstar (route #4, above), there are two obvious black streaks. Flabob heads straight up the face between the two streaks.

SUPERSTAR SLAB

6. **THE BLACK STREAK**   **5.10+**

A prominent block overhangs the center of Superstar Slab, an
there is an obvious black streak on the rock immediately belo
this block.   Start a few feet to the right of this streak, the
climb up and left — generally following the streak up to t
block, which can be passed on the left.

7. **THE WATERCHUTE**   **5.8**

Ascend the obvious waterchute to the right of the bl
described in route #6 above.

NOTE: To the right of the waterchute, there are a variety of s
face climbs; difficulty of 5.5 and up.

CAUTION: There's lots of poison oak around Superstar Slab.

127

THE TRIANGLES

THE TRIANGLES are an aptly named formation of three large triangularly-shaped blocks, with the blocks positioned such that they form two distinct cracks. Though the climbs are short and have been done as boulder problems, they should be top-roped for safety's sake.

1.   LEFT FACE   5.10

Start at a pair of nice fingerholds near the center of the left triangle. Proceed straight up and mantle over the top.

2.   RIGHT FACE   5.10

Start about three feet to the left of the triangle's right-hand edge. The route curves up and right, always maintaining about the same distance from the edge.

3.   TRIANGLE CHIMNEY   5.3

Climb as a layback till the angle steepens. At this point, transfer into the crack and finish using chimney technique. This is an ideal climb for beginners to practice both layback and chimney technique.

4.   THE SICKLE   5.2

This is the right-hand crack; it's a comparatively easy layback.

5.   WALKATHON   5.7

This short climb is on the face immediately right of route #5. It's tempting to make use of the edge; however, this should be avoided.

6.   SLEEPATHON   5.10+

Mantle onto the small hold about three feet to the left of this block's right-hand edge. Make one friction move above and the top can be reached.

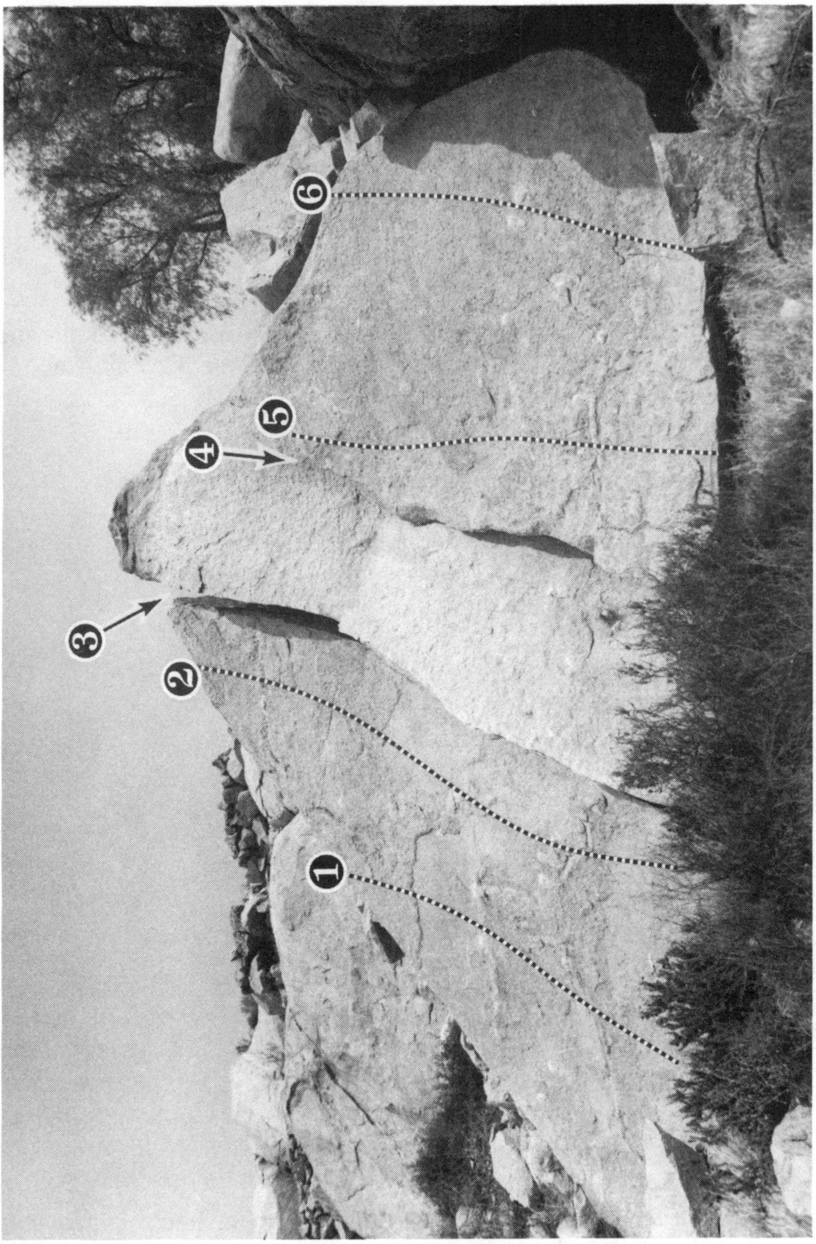

THE TRIANGLES

ENGLISH SMOOTH SOLE SLAB

The ENGLISH SMOOTH SOLE SLAB is an impressive block that has several classic face climbs. Though the face is seemingly completely smooth, there's an abundance of thin fingerholds. The Jamcrack Route which adjoins the slab is reputed to be the most popular climb at Mount Rubidoux.

1. **THE JAMCRACK**   5.2

The Jamcrack is a forty-foot crack which forms the left-hand edge of the English Smooth Sole Slab. The 5.2 rating allows the use of holds on the adjoining face — the climb is much more awkward if the crack alone is used.

2. **SMOOTH SOLE CENTER**   5.10+

Begin at the center of the slab and proceed generally straight up; the most frequently climbed variation bends slightly to the left.

3. **SMOOTH SOLE RIGHT**   5.10+

Begin just right of the center and climb straight up till it is possible to step right into a shallow trough. Either exit left or follow the trough to the top.

4. **TRIPLE CRACK LEFT**   5.7

This is the short flared crack located about fifteen feet to the right of the Smooth Sole Slab.

5. **TRIPLE CRACK CENTER**   5.9

This is the thin crack a few feet to the right of route #4.

6. **TRIPLE CRACK RIGHT**   5.7

The third and final crack is a left-curving layback; it's located a few feet to the right of the center crack.

ENGLISH SMOOTH SOLE SLAB
Note: Routes 4 - 6 are not pictured;
They are located about 15 feet to the right.

JOE BROWN BOULDER

JOE BROWN is a large rounded boulder that has become one of the most popular climbing sites at Mount Rubidoux. It's covered with flakes and holds, and it can be climbed almost anywhere. There are routes for everyone, from the complete beginner to the competitive climber. Because of the abundance of potential climbs, the routes described here are necessarily limited to just a few of the best (and the most obvious).

At one point in time, there was a guard rail across the top of this boulder. Though the railing is gone, several of the iron posts remain — and these make excellent belay anchors.

1. **ZIG-ZAG**   5.1

   Begin at a point about ten feet left of the prominent water-chute (see route #4). "Zig" up and left to a flake, which "zags" back right and up to the top.

2. **FACE**   5.6

   Start from the same point as route #1, but proceed pretty much straight up the face.

3. **FACE**   5.6

   Climb straight up the face a few feet to the left of the water-chute of route #4.

4. **WATERSTREAK CORNER**   5.7

   On the west face of Joe Brown Boulder there is a prominent and easily-identified waterchute. Climb straight up the chute and exit to the right a few feet from the top.

5. **SMALL BROWN**   5.10

   Start a few feet right of the waterchute (route #4, above), and climb to a small ledge about eight feet off the ground. From the ledge, reach up and right to a thin flake. Follow the flake to a small pocket and easier climbing above.

JOE BROWN BOULDER

6. **CYCLOPS**   **5.10+**

To the right of Small Brown (route #5, above), an orange band angles up and right. Follow this band to the "Cyclops" — a circular depression in the rock. Several variations exist above, and the top can be reached by proceeding left, right, or straight up.

7. **POWER PACK**   **5.11+**

A few feet to the right of the "Cyclops" (see route #6), there is a four-foot wide grey streak on the rock. Power Pack proceeds up the right-hand edge of this streak. The crux involves negotiating the sizeable overhang above.

NOTE: In addition to the seven climbs pictured and described above, a variety of face climbs can be found to the right of Power Pack. These range from 5.10 (immediately right of Power Pack) to 5.2 (on the extreme right edge of the boulder).

Jean Fradette on English Smooth Sole Slab

HALF DOME

1. **LEFT CRACK**   **5.8**

2. **RIGHT CRACK**   **5.8**

HALF DOME is located slightly downhill from JOE BROWN BOULDER. Its vertical north face has two obvious cracks, both of which are very popular climbs. Though both cracks are rated 5.8, the right crack is generally acknowledged to be slightly more difficult.

A belay can be established utilizing the anchoring bolt on top.

THE ISLAND

THE ISLAND is located on the southwest summit of Mount Rubidoux. It has both easy access and classic routes, and it is the site of considerable climbing activity. The better routes, however, tend to be the more difficult ones. A few easy climbs have been included for the sake of completeness, but they are short and unimpressive. THE ISLAND is thus recommended primarily for the more experienced climber.

1. **WHITE BOOK**   **5.10**

    A left-facing open book can be found around the corner on the south side of The Island. The open book leans to the right — and that's the direction of this route.

2. **K.P.'S ARETE**   **5.11+**

    This route follows the obvious prow of The Island's left corner. Formerly an aid route, it has been done free by making use of the numerous thin cracks.

3. **BOOTLEG CRACK (FLAKE CRACK) 5.3**

    Ascend the obvious crack which has been formed by the breaking away of a large flake.

4. **HUNCHBACK**   **5.0**

    Climb the easy crack on the right edge of the flake which forms route #3. It's located a few feet up the obvious gulley.

5. **SILVERSTONE**   **5.11+**

    Ascend a series of small cups up and right, starting at a point about four feet to the right of an obvious black streak.

6. **TEFLON**   **5.11+**

    A partially-formed alcove can be found directly at the point of The Island's most pronounced overhang. Ascend the face to the left of the thin crack found in this alcove.

7. **IN THE PICTURE**   **5.11**

The start is the same as for Quasimodo (route #8, below); however, exit to the face above before turning the corner.

8. **QUASIMODO**   **5.11**

This route follows the obvious and prominent arch. Start in the right-hand corner and layback/undercling the arch up and left. The arch can be exited at a variety of points, or it can be climbed all the way to the exit for Silverstone (route #5, above).

9. **5.9er**   **5.10**

Start in the thin crack just right of the obvious route #8.
Follow this crack to reach face climbing up and to the right.

10. **WHOOPEE CRACK**   **5.7/5.4**

Climb the flake/pedestal to the right of route #9. The left crack is 5.7; the curving right crack is 5.4.

THE ISLAND

19

BIG ROCK

BIG ROCK is a partial dome of high quality granitic rock. It's located on the shore of Lake Perris (southeast of Riverside), and it is readily accessible as a day outing for climbers coming from Los Angeles and Orange Counties.

BIG ROCK's primary attraction is difficult friction face climbing, and it features routes of up to 165 feet in length. A few routes can be top-roped; however, most are climbed on lead. Protection is provided by more than 100 bolts. Though there has been some recent bolt chopping, most routes are still reasonably well protected.

ACCESS

It's possible to either park outside the yellow gate on Bernasconi Beach Road or to utilize the beach's parking lot. Parking outside the gate saves the parking fee, plus it allows climbers to stay past the beach's 6 p.m. closure. On the other hand, there has been a rash of vandalism in recent years, and a car parked outside the gate is at risk of being broken into.

From the gate, walk or drive about 1/4 mile up Bernasconi Beach Road to an entrance kiosk. If driving, park at entrance lot. Hike up the paved road on the left immediately past the entrance station. BIG ROCK is the obvious partial dome about 3/4 mile up this side road.

DESCENT

It is possible to rappel off some routes, but most climbers typically descend on foot. The left-hand walk-off (see photo) is direct, but exposed. The right-hand walk-off is easier; however, it has the disadvantage of heading through an abundance of poison oak.

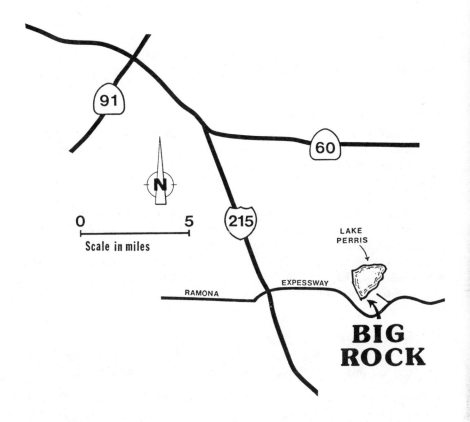

DIRECTIONS

Take either the 10, 60, or 91 Freeway east to the 215 Freeway South. After passing March Air Force Base, watch for the Ramona Expressway exit. From this exit, take the Ramona Expressway east approximately 6.5 miles (past the Lake Perris dam and a large rock outcrop on the left) to Bernasconi Road. Turn left onto Bernasconi Road and park either outside the obvious gate or proceed to the pay-parking lot.

NOTE: It is very likely that if you enter the park, your vehicle will be checked for a parking receipt — don't get caught without one. Also, the park service is prompt about locking the gate at the posted closing hour.

CLIMBING ROUTES

1. **EDGER SANCTION**   **5.10A**
    Ascend the smooth face a few feet left of the first major crack on BIG ROCK's north side. Climb to double bolts; rappel or walk-off (exposed).

2. **ENGLISH HANGING GARDENS**   **5.11B**
    There is a low roof near the north edge of the climbing formation. Surmount this roof on broken black rock, and follow the trough above. Crux is at bottom.

3. **RAW DEAL**   **5.11B**
    Traverse right on a short ramp to the right of Route #2. Follow bolts up and left to a thin flake, then follow flake up and right to a diagonal crack.

4. **GIANT STEP**   **5.10C**
    Follow bolt line 10-15 feet left of Northwest Passage (Route #5).

5. **NORTHWEST PASSAGE**   **5.9**
    Climb face directly below the left edge of a prominent roof, bypass this roof on the left, and continue to belay bolts above.

6. **THE ROOF**   **5.9**
    Climb face up to and over the prominent roof, then proceed to belay ledge above. Common descent is to traverse right and rappel off double bolts, or continue up via the Left Flake (Route A).

7. **BOOGALOO**   **5.8 (5.9)**
    Start in obvious depression, angle up and right to an elliptical hole, then follow bolts towards Right Flake (Route B). The 5.9 variation bypasses the elliptical hole by climbing straight up out of the depression.

8. **WEDUNETT**   **5.6**
    A ramp angles up and left from The Trough (see Route #10). Ascend this about 25 feet to an obvious hole. Follow bolts above to a belay stance (up and left of large pocket).

BIG ROCK

141

9. **CRATER MAKER**   5.7

Ascend first line of bolts to left of The Trough (see Route #10). Climb ends at belay bolts of Route #8.

10. **THE TROUGH**   5.5

Follow obvious water chute near center of main face. A 165 foot rope is required to complete route in one pitch. A 150 foot rope reaches a belay stance in a bucket, but this requires a short second pitch.

11. **AFRICAN FLAKE**   5.5 (5.6)

About 15 feet right of The Trough (Route #10), there's an orange flake shaped vaguely like the continent of Africa. Pass this flake on its right, then angle up and right to the belay bolts of Routes 12, 13, & 14. African Flake continues up and left to the bucket belay stance of The Trough. The 5.6 variation proceeds straight up from the start, thereby bypassing the above-mentioned bolts of Routes 12, 13, & 14.

12. **FRONTAL LOBOTOMY**   5.10A

There are three short bolt routes to the right of African Flake (Route #11). The three are commonly climbed as a combination — ascend one to set up a belay, then top-rope the remaining two. Frontal Lobotomy is the first of the three; it's about 15 feet right of African Flake. From the belay bolts, either continue up via African Flake, or rappel off.

13. **MIND BENDER**   5.9

This is the bolt route about 10 feet right of Frontal Lobotomy (see Route #12).

14. **PUDNURTLE**   5.8

This is the bolt route about 20 feet right of Frontal Lobotomy (see Route #12).

15. **PUPPY DOG**   5.6

Follow the bolt route about 20 feet right of Pudnurtle (see route #14). NOTE: Some bolts have been chopped and the route gets pretty lead-out. Also, be aware that there is poison oak around the base of this climb.

16. **HARD TROUGH**   **5.8**
Ascend a line of bolts which head up the waterchute near south edge of climbing formation. Poison oak at base.

17. **HEADWALL**   **5.9**
Ascend the bolt line about 20 feet right of The Hard Trough (see Route #16). Poison oak at base.

UPPER CLIMBING ROUTES

The Upper Routes are typically reached by climbing one of Routes 6 - 9 to reach a belay ledge.

A.   **LEFT FLAKE**   **5.6**
Lieback crack in the corner of the obvious left-hand flake. Chocks required.

B.   **RIGHT FLAKE**   **5.7**
Lieback crack in corner of obvious right-hand flake.   Chocks required.

C.   **MAD DOGS**   **5.10D**
Ascend line of bolts which follow black streak to right of Route B.

D.   **CHEAP THRILLS**   **5.10A**
Ascend line of bolts about 6 - 8 feet right of Route C.

20

TAHQUITZ

Like JOSHUA TREE, TAHQUITZ hardly needs an introduction — many climbers consider it to be the finest Southern California site. TAHQUITZ (or Lily Rock as it is sometimes called) is a massive dome-like crag in the San Jacinto mountains. It lies on the western slope of Tahquitz Peak, and it dominates the landscape above the nearby resort town of Idyllwild.

TAHQUITZ features prominently in the climbing history of North America. The first routes were put up by the Rock Climbing Section of the Sierra Club in 1936 — a time when California climbing was just beginning. More importantly, TAHQUITZ played a central role in the climbing revolution of the 1950's. During that period, the common rating standard now known as the Yosemite Decimal System was developed primarily at TAHQUITZ.

(continued on page 146)

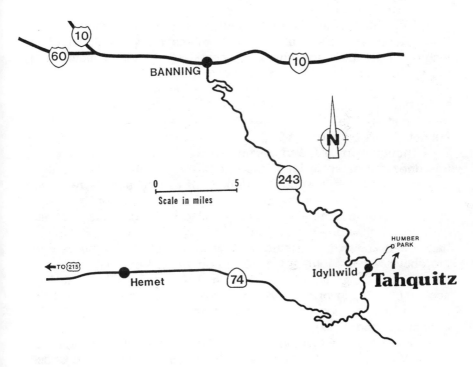

DIRECTIONS

From Highway 215 (southeast of Riverside), take Highway 74 east thirty-two miles (passing through Hemet) to its intersection with Highway 243. Take 243 left to the resort town of Idyllwild. Alternatively, Idyllwild can be reached by taking 243 south from Banning, which is located east of Redlands on I-10.

From the center of Idyllwild, take North Circle Drive approximately one mile to its intersection with South Circle Drive. Turn right onto South Circle, then make an immediate left onto Fern Valley Road. Park just past the Humber Park entrance sign.

The summit of TAHQUITZ is at an elevation of about 8,000 feet. This means that the best climbing seasons are Spring, Summer, and Fall. Though TAHQUITZ can be climbed in Winter, there is typically snow and ice present during that season. The area's high elevation places it in a climatic zone that is dominated by White Fir, Yellow Pine, and other conifers. The setting is idyllic, and the cool mountain environment adds greatly to the pleasures of climbing at TAHQUITZ.

TAHQUITZ is the closest thing to Yosemite-like conditions in all of Southern California. It offers routes of up to 900 feet in length, all of which are multi-pitch lead climbs. Approximately 100 routes have been established; these range in technical difficulty from 5.0 to 5.12. Individual routes typically involve a variety of climbing techniques, including both face and crack. The rock is very hard and granite-like (it's actually quartz diorite), and holds are usually — but not always — secure.

Though many of the routes on TAHQUITZ are technically easy, this does not mean to imply that the site is suitable for beginners. Since most routes are long, a degree of commitment is required. Furthermore, difficulties in route finding are frequently encountered, and it is easy to stray into harder climbing than anticipated. Route finding can slow down a climbing party, and inexperienced climbers have been known to get stuck on the rock overnight. And as if all the above is not enough, it needs to be pointed out that numerous serious accidents have occurred on TAHQUITZ. The first fatal accident (1959) involved a victim of rockfall from above — and the 1959 incident is not the only rockfall fatality. In short, TAHQUITZ is a serious undertaking.

Detailed climbing information can be found in other guidebooks. Randy Vogel's *Rock Climbs of Tahquitz and Suicide Rocks* and Chuck Wilts' *Tahquitz and Suicide Rocks* are particularly recommended. Since so much information is already available, only a few routes are presented in the following pages. The intent here — as elsewhere in this book — is just to introduce the area to the first-time visitor.

ACCESS

Just past the Humber Park entrance sign, take the Ernie Maxwell Scenic Trail. This dips down to a stream crossing (sometimes dry), and then cuts sharply to the west. Proceeding along this trail, various scrambleways appear to the left. These all lead to TAHQUITZ. The best one, however, starts near a solitary boulder (to the left of the trail) about 300 yards past the stream crossing. This particular scrambleway leads directly to Lunch Rock. It's a steep uphill hike, and it takes about 40 minutes from Humber Park.

LUNCH ROCK

Lunch Rock is a key landmark useful in locating routes on TAHQUITZ's northwest face (i.e., the routes described below). If the above directions are followed, Lunch Rock is easy to find; it can be identified by the Stokes litter kept in the vicinity.

DESCENT

A friction descent may be made down TAHQUITZ's south face; however, this is exposed and may be difficult to find. An easier (though more roundabout) descent involves scrambling to the very top of the rock formation. The view from the top is definitely worth the extra time required to pass that way.

From the top, drop down to the saddle to the east. Various scrambleways head down in the general direction of the south face. Whenever a choice presents itself, bear to the right — thus keeping close to the rock. This scrambleway eventually reaches the West Buttress and continues on to Lunch Rock.

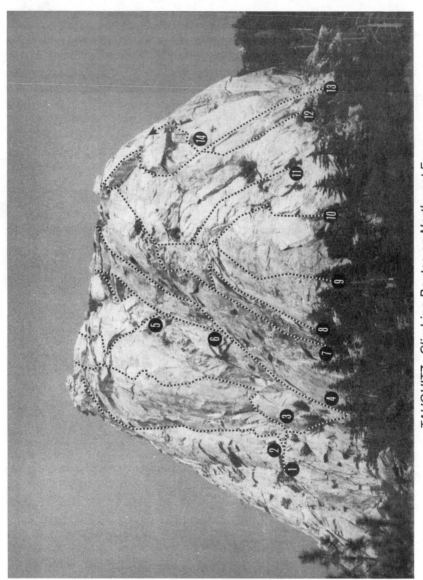

TAHQUITZ, Climbing Routes on Northwest Face

CLIMBING ROUTES:

TAHQUITZ'S NORTHWEST FACE

1. FROM BAD TRAVERSE 4th Class

This traverse is used to get to the start of Super Pooper and The Vampire (Routes 2 & 3). From the top of the 1st pitch of The Trough (Route 4), angle up and left, climbing past several trees. The traverse continues to the large ledge atop an obvious 150 foot buttress (and beyond); however, the starts to Routes 2 & 3 are reached just before this buttress. Though frequently described as 4th Class, there is a very short 5th Class section near the end.

2. SUPER POOPER 5.10A

Super Pooper follows the prominent cleft which angles up and left, starting at a point just right of the 150 foot buttress described in Route #1 above. Enter this cleft at its base, and follow it up to the crux (protected by a fixed pin). Easier climbing leads to a roof above, which is passed on the left. On the last pitch, a vertical headwall appears to block further progress; however, a way up can be found by traversing to the right.

3. THE VAMPIRE 5.11A

This climb is considered by some to be the finest climb at TAHQUITZ. The easiest approach is via "From Bad Traverse" (Route #1). From near the end of this traverse, climb a short 5.7 crack, then traverse right and down to reach the obvious "Bat Crack." Jam and lieback this crack, which gradually narrows as it heads up the right-facing open book. The second pitch traverses left past two bolts to reach a left-curving flake. Continue up flakes till it's possible to traverse left to reach a bolt belay. The third pitch returns to the flake and continues up till it's possible to transfer to a left-angling dihedral above. The final pitch leads to an obvious notch above.

Routes 1 - 6

4. THE TROUGH   5.0

The Trough is the easiest 5th class route at TAHQUITZ, and it is accordingly appropriate for beginners. The Trough is the obvious gully that diagonals up and right across TAHQUITZ's NW Face, starting at a point about 75 yards left of Lunch Rock. From Lunch Rock, walk directly up to the main rock face, and traverse left about 100 feet (passing by the start of Angel's Fright — Route 7). Pass through a short squeeze chimney behind a tree, and traverse about 75 feet further left to reach a small buttress. Scramble up and left over broken rock to reach the crack which starts The Trough. Roped climbing starts at this crack — follow it up as it gradually widens into an obvious trough. Two or three pitches lead to Pine Tree Ledge, which is reached via a short right-leaning lieback flake. From this ledge, one or two pitches of mixed 3rd/4th class leads up and right to a prominent tree, which marks the end of roped climbing.

5. UPPER ROYAL ARCH   5.7

Climb The Trough (Route 4) to Pine Tree Ledge, then ascend the first pitch of Piton Pooper (Route 6). Shortly thereafter, take the prominent crack which angles up and left to a tree at the righthand corner of the Upper Arch. Continue under the arch until it is necessary to transfer onto the adjoining face. Ascend the overhang at the top of the arch; from here, a short 5.7 pitch completes the climb.

6. PITON POOPER   5.7

Ascend The Trough (Route 4) to Pine Tree Ledge. From the ledge, traverse left to a crack in a left-facing open book. Follow this crack past a fixed pin, then stay close to the curving righthand wall. Continue up to the prominent block above, which can be passed on either the left or right.

7.   ANGEL'S FRIGHT   5.4

Angel's Fright is one of the most popular of the easier climbs
at TAHQUITZ.   It has only two short sections of 5.4, thus
it'ssuitable for most beginners.   To reach Angel's Fright, head
directly up from Lunch Rock and traverse about 75 feet to the
left.   The climb starts in a short 5.2 chimney, which leads to
Litter Ledge.   Above Litter Ledge, climb the obvious crack (or
the face to its right) to reach a 4th class trough.   This trough
ends at an overhanging bulge, which is passed on the right
(5.4).   Twenty feet above is Lunch Ledge.   Several variations
are possible from this ledge.   The easiest (5.1) heads up past
large steps and brush to reach a long right-angling ramp.   The
overhang at the top of this ramp is passed on the right.   A
more difficult (5.6), but more direct variation ascends the lieback flake directly above Lunch Ledge.

8.   HUMAN FRIGHT   5.10A

Human Fright parallels Angel's Fright (Route 7).   From a point
about 30 feet to the right of the chimney of Angel's Fright,
follow an obvious crack in the corner of a right-facing dihedral
(this is further identified by being just left of a large fir tree).
Two pitches lead to a ledge adjacent to Angel's Fright.   Either
continue via Angel's Fright or rap off.

9.   BLANKETTY BLANK   5.10C

From Lunch Rock, head straight up to the rock face and
traverse right.   At the point where the ground starts to drop
off to the right, look for the start of Blanketty Blank a few
feet below.   Ascend a blank face up and right to a fixed pin.
(This pin is four feet left of and a foot above a small bush
growing in a horizontal crack.)   From the fixed pin, follow the
flake above as it curves up and left to a bolted belay stance.
Continue up past a shallow left-facing corner to a second
bolted belay stance.   Proceed pretty much straight up to join
the Fingertrip route at Fingertrip Arch.

Angel's Fright and Human Fright

10.   FINGERTRIP   5.7

About 50 yards right of Lunch Rock, a large slab leans against the main face.   Look for a crack in the corner of a left-facing open book a few feet further right.   Climb this open book (straying occasionally onto the the adjoining face) to reach a ledge with a large fir tree.   Above the tree, lieback/jam a crack past two blocks.   Continue up, then left to a belay stance below the obvious Fingertrip arch.   Surmount this overhang near its left end; easier climbing leads up and left to Lunch Ledge. Continue as described in Route 7.

*The 3rd Class Gully and Oak Tree which form
the start of Fingertip Traverse*

11. FINGERTIP TRAVERSE   5.3

Fingertip Traverse has a truly unique start (see below), plus it offers quality climbing with great exposure — it's thus a highly popular climb. It's located around the corner to the left of Jensen's Jaunt (see Route #13). Scramble up the 3rd class gully to reach a medium-sized oak tree. Climb this tree's topmost section, then transfer left to the rock. Follow an easy crack up as it gradually widens into a trough which ends at the "Jungle" (a bushy ledge). From the lower left end of the "Jungle," lieback the obvious flake which curves up and left. As this flake tapers out, a delicate step to the left leads to a belay protected by two fixed pins. The next pitch heads up the namesake traverse — a crack which angles up and left past two bushes. After the traverse, follow broken rock up and left to Lunch Ledge. Continue from this ledge as described in Route 7.

Nathan Warstler hanging out on The Fingertip Traverse

12. COFFIN NAIL   5.7

Third class climbing leads to a prominent alcove to the left of
Jensen's Jaunt (see Route #13). Follow the crack which starts
in the rear of this alcove, and stay in it as it gradually merges
into a right-facing dihedral. Continue up, following the dihedral as it angles up and right. Exit via a thin crack which
leads to Jensen's Jaunt (which is followed from this point on).

13. JENSEN'S JAUNT   5.6

This route starts from the extreme western corner of
TAHQUITZ. Ascend broken rock to a left-leaning dihedral (to
the left side of the rock's sharp corner). At the top of this
dihedral, work around the left corner of the huge block above.
Continue along the left side of this block to a corner, where
it's possible to climb up unto it. Steep unprotected friction
leads to the top.

14. TRAITOR HORN   5.8

Ascend the dihedral of Route 13 to the base of the huge overhanging block above. Traverse right along a narrow crack to
reach Traitor Horn (so named because it's not the horn which
forms the crux of the route). Continue traversing right to a
small platform, then climb up into the alcove at the base of
the true horn. Traverse right to the horn, and — once it's
gained — stand on it to reach the ridge above. Alternatively,
the horn can be bypassed via the deep crack to its left. Once
above the horn, steep friction leads to the end of the route.

Routes 12 - 14

21

SUICIDE

SUICIDE is the companion climbing formation to TAHQUITZ. The former is located directly across Strawberry Valley from the latter. Since there is good camping facilities in the nearby village of Idyllwild, climbers typically spend more than one day in the area — thus having the opportunity to visit both sites in one outing.

SUICIDE was not developed as a climbing site till the mid-60's, and it only became popular after the 1970 edition of Chuck Wilts' *Tahquitz Guide* included routes for this newer area. Though SUICIDE came to attention later, it has now caught up with TAHQUITZ in popularity. In fact, many climbers now prefer SUICIDE to its larger companion. This is due to a variety of factors. For starters, SUICIDE has an easier approach (about twenty minutes as compared to TAHQUITZ's forty). Furthermore, routes at SUICIDE are shorter (the longest are about 400 feet), thus allowing climbers to complete several in a day. Finally, SUICIDE features classic friction face climbing of a type that is not found on TAHQUITZ.

Virtually all routes on SUICIDE are lead climbs. Many are bolted; however, chocks are required for others. Climbers should thus bring a standard rack of hardware. Well over 100 climbs have been recorded, and route information is included in the guidebooks mentioned in the preceding section on TAHQUITZ. Since so much route information is already available, the presentation here is quite limited. As at TAHQUITZ, the intent is only to introduce this site to the first-time visitor.

ACCESS

From the parking area (see map & directions), take the climber's trail which dips down to a small stream west of the road. This trail is fairly obvious, and it is marked by a small sign. Cross the stream to reach a paved road on the opposite side. Hike up the road about 300 yards to reach a climber's path, which is also marked by signs. From this point, 15 minutes of vigorous hiking leads to the base of "Weeping Wall."

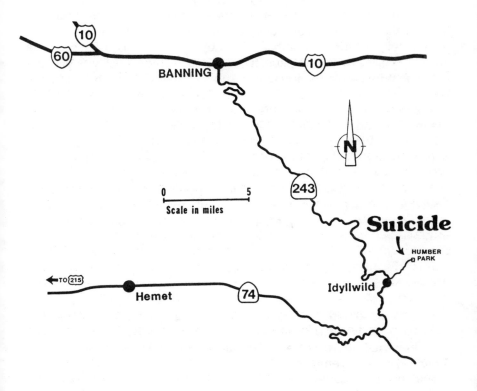

DIRECTIONS

From Highway 215 (southeast of Riverside), take Highway 74 east thirty-two miles (passing through Hemet) to its intersection with Highway 243. Take 243 left to the resort town of Idyllwild. Alternatively, Idyllwild can be reached by taking 243 south from Banning, which is located east of Redlands on I-10.

From the center of Idyllwild, take North Circle Drive approximately one mile to its intersection with South Circle Drive. Turn right onto South Circle, then take an immediate left onto Fern Valley Road. There is a small parking turnout for SUICIDE ROCK on the left, about 1½ miles up Fern Valley Road. The turnout is directly opposite two large water tanks, and these make good landmarks to help locate the SUICIDE trail.

WEEPING WALL

"Weeping Wall" is located near the center of SUICIDE ROCK. It's a 300 foot slab that contains many fine face climbs, and it is one of the most popular walls at SUICIDE. Notable climbing areas to the left include "Smooth Sole Slab" and "Sunshine Face." The former has several one-pitch face routes of high quality, while the latter features hard face climbs of up to three pitches in length. In addition, many fine routes can be found to the north (right) of "Weeping Wall." Among others, these northerly routes include two decent beginner's climbs: "Tabby Treat" (5.1) and "Little Murders" (5.3). "Tabby Treat" ascends a large and obvious left-facing dihedral, and "Little Murders" ascends the right-facing open book about 60 feet further north.

"Weeping Wall" is not only highly popular, it's also an excellent introduction to the type of climbing found at SUICIDE. Accordingly, it's the only area for which detailed route information is presented here.

DESCENT

The most direct descent of "Weeping Wall" involves a rappel into "Bye Gully" at the left margin of the wall. "Bye Gully" is rated 5.5; however, there is only one 5th class section — a short flaring chimney. The remainder of the gully is only 3rd class; thus its popularity as a descent route.

A more circuitous (but easier) descent involves hiking up to and around the northern portion of SUICIDE ROCK.

"WEEPING WALL" CLIMBING ROUTES

1.   COMMENCEMENT   5.9

On the left-hand edge of Weeping Wall, a long thin slab lies against the wall. This can be climbed on its face (unprotected) or as a layback along the right edge (both variations are 5.6). From the slab's top, angle up — first to the right, then left to an obvious flake. No bolts on route. 2 pitches.

"WEEPING WALL", SUICIDE ROCK

2. CLAM CHOWDER 5.9

Climb the left side of Weeping Wall (about ten feet right of the slab of Route #1) to the belay bolts on Surprise (see Route #3). Continue straight up for fifty feet, then angle left to a rib which is followed to a belay ledge. Climb to the tree above. 3 pitches.

3. SURPRISE 5.8

Begin near a small fir tree, and parallel a short crack. Continue up and left on a long exposed runout to a belay ledge. Traverse to the right edge of this ledge, and climb past a bolt which protects the crux. Easier climbing leads first to a lieback crack, then left to the base of a prominent trough. Follow this trough to summit. 3 pitches.

4. DUCK SOUP 5.10C

From the crack which starts Surprise (see Route #3), proceed pretty much straight up; Surprise's belay ledge is passed on the right. 3 pitches.

5. REVELATION 5.10A

From the crack which starts Surprise (see Route #3), angle up and right to the third bolt on Serpentine (see Route #6). The route then angles slightly left to a belay below an obvious shallow dihedral. After bypassing the dihedral, the next two pitches ascend pretty much straight up the face above. 3 pitches.

6. SERPENTINE 5.9

Serpentine starts near a large oak tree, which is located at the right-hand edge of Weeping Wall. The route angles up and left past three bolts (the third is shared with Revelation — see Route #5). From this shared bolt, Serpentine angles up and right to a belay stance. The climb continues straight up, then up and right to the next belay. 3 pitches.

7.   **TEN KARAT GOLD**   5.10a

Start from the small ledge at the base of the obvious Sampson, Goliath, and David (Routes 8, 9, & 10, below). From the left side of this ledge, follow a dike up and left, then diagonal sharply back right to a wide grey streak. Follow this up past a fixed pin, then up and right to a belay stance. Traverse right to a small ledge, then proceed straight up on almost featureless rock. 2 pitches.

8.   **SAMPSON (Not Pictured)**   5.9

Sampson follows the obvious left-facing dihedral which forms the right margin of Weeping Wall. It is strenuous, difficult to protect, and ends with an awkward 5.9 mantle. 2 pitches.

9.   **GOLIATH (Not Pictured)**   5.7

Goliath follows the obvious flaring chimney to the right of Sampson (see Route #8). Awkward 2 pitches.

10. **DAVID (Not pictured)**   5.7

David is the smaller crack just right of Goliath (see Route #9). The crux is getting from the chimney into this crack. 1 or 2 pitches.

11. **REBOLTING DEVELOPMENT**   5.11A

This is the bolt route which goes up the smooth face between David (route #10) and Delila (Route #12). It's about twenty feet to the left of Delila. 3 pitches.

12. **DELILA**   5.8

Delila is the right-facing open book about 50 feet right of David (see Route #10). 2 pitches.

22

THE BEACH

Located in Corona del Mar, "The Beach" (as it is known to climbers) is the most popular climbing site in all of Orange County. THE BEACH consists of a long curving formation, with climbing routes extending to a height of about 45 feet. Some of the higher ones might best be top-roped, but most can be accomplished without roping—the sandy beach makes for reasonably safe landings.

Vogel's *Hunk Guide to Orange County* lists a total of 51 climbs at THE BEACH, and this guide should be consulted by anyone desiring specifics. THE BEACH, however, is primarily a bouldering site, and individual climbs are not listed here. Merely look for the chalk marks to find the popular bouldering problems.

A bit of caution is in order: the rock is fine-grained sandstone, and — though generally sound — it is, of course, subject to breakage. Furthermore, holds are frequently damp and slippery due to the closeness of the ocean (a matter of only a few feet).

Overall, THE BEACH is a highly recommended climbing site. It is worth a long drive to experience the unique pleasure of combining a day of bouldering with more traditional beach activities (tanning and swimming — to name the most obvious).

DIRECTIONS

Take the San Diego Freeway (405) toward Newport Beach, exit onto Highway 73, and continue into Corona del Mar. At the intersection of MacArthur and Pacific Coast Highway (1), turn left onto PCH and continue a short distance to Marguerite. Turn right on Marguerite and follow it to a "T" intersection at Ocean Blvd. Make another right onto Ocean. The entrance to Corona del Mar State Beach is two blocks ahead on the left. The state beach parking lot requires a fee; however, it may be possible to find parking on the street (not too likely on weekends). The bouldering area is on the far side of the rocks just north of the parking lot.

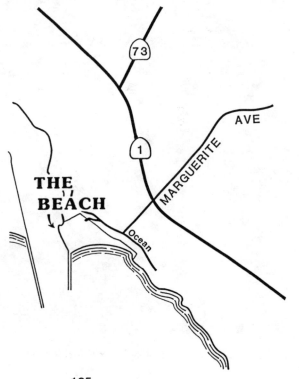

Phil Calvert bouldering at The Beach

NOTE:

There is some uncertainty as to the legality of climbing at THE BEACH. The authors made a check and were informed that climbing is permissible. However, there have been numerous incidents of climbing being "discouraged" by the police and/or lifeguards. The main problem appears to be that a few climbers have not respected the rights of sunbathers. If you choose to visit The Beach, the authors recommend checking with local officials, and—above all—please be courteous to others.

23

THE FALLS

"The Falls" is the collective name for a large and spread-out area of granite boulders. The site features seemingly endless bouldering opportunities, a variety of top-roped climbs, and a few possibilities for lead climbing. Though THE FALLS actually lies in Riverside County, it is included in Vogel's *Hunk Guide To Orange County* (because the majority of the climbers visiting the site are from Orange County metropolitan areas). Vogel's book should thus be consulted by anyone desiring more detailed information on the available climbing.

In the winter, ample water flows over the waterfall, making the area quite scenic. THE FALLS thus appeals to partiers as well as climbers, and there is an unfortunate abundance of trash and broken bottles. Climbers should be aware that the broken glass can pose a bouldering hazard (especially with respect to dangerous landings). Climbers should further be aware that there is an abundance of poison oak — particularly in the lower canyon near the stream and also around the waterfall.

There is a large turnout on Highway 74 adjacent to the Falls. From the turnout, various scrambleways lead down to the water, and it is only a pleasant 5 - 10 minute hike to the climbing sites.

DIRECTIONS

From Los Angeles or San Diego:

Take Interstate 5 to San Juan Capistrano and exit onto the Ortega Highway (74). Look for a Cleveland National Forest Campground, which is approximately 18 miles east on 74. Two miles further, and there's a large turnout on the right. Park here; "The Falls" is below the highway to the west (left).

From Riverside:

Take the Corona Expressway (15), and turn west on Highway 74 (toward Lake Elsinore). From this intersection, drive approximately 12 miles. The turnout/parking area will be on the left.

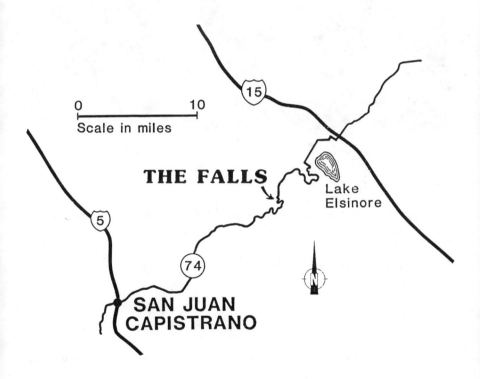

OVERVIEW OF THE FALLS

Overall view of The Falls as seen from Highway 74. Arrowed climbing sites are:

A)   Ziggy Boulder: Split by two main seams; the left is 5.9, the right is 5.7.

B)   This pinnacle-like standing boulder has two *thin* cracks on its main face; the left is 5.10, the right is 5.8, A4.

C)   Elephant Boulder (not visible in photograph): See following pages.

D)   The Falls: See following pages.

ELEPHANT BOULDER

CLIMBING ROUTES: ELEPHANT BOULDER

Elephant Boulder is the first large boulder downstream from the waterfall (left-hand side as seen facing downstream). It is a good and clean granite boulder, and it offers the following top-roped climbs:

1)   5.2

2)   5.10

3)   5.10

4)   5.8

CLIMBING ROUTES: THE WATERFALL

    Several challenging climbs can be found on the granite face immediately to the left of the waterfall (the feature for which the overall climbing site is named).   For the most part, the climbs follow crack systems which are capable of accepting protection. However, access to the routes is a little tricky (see below), and it is therefore recommended that a secure top-rope belay be established before attempting these climbs. A good belay position can be found high above the water (see photograph). You'll need a good supply of webbing — the best protection is a ways back from the edge.

    A noteworthy feature of these climbs is that they rise straight up from a shallow pool (this is the feature that makes for tricky access). If a secure top-rope belay has been established, the climbs can be safely approached from the sloping ledge to the left of the first climb. From this ledge, you can make either a nervy traverse or equally nervy pendulum over to the route of your choice.

THE ROUTES:

1)	5.7
2)	5.9
3)	5.10
4)	5.10
5)	5.10+

MAIN CLIMBING AREA

24

MOUNT WOODSON

MOUNT WOODSON is generally acknowledged to be the best climbing site in the San Diego area, and this reputation is well-deserved. Located in the rugged hills of San Diego County northeast of the city, MOUNT WOODSON features a truly impressive array of boulders. The rock is high quality fine-grained granite, and the boulders have an abundance of difficult cracks and thin flakes. Moreover, the boulders tend to be larger than those found at other sites, and many routes range up to 40 feet in length. Most routes can be top-roped, but leading and free soloing are also common.

MOUNT WOODSON is obviously readily accessible from the San Diego area. But it is becoming increasingly popular, and many climbers consider this site to be worth a long drive (it's about two hours from Los Angeles). This is especially true for more experienced climbers, as the primary attractions are the long and difficult cracks (these are generally 5.10 or harder). A sampling of climbs of lesser difficulty are included here; however, MOUNT WOODSON has only limited appeal for anyone not interested in serious climbing.

The routes recommended in the following pages are intended to serve only as an introduction to MOUNT WOODSON. More than 400 routes have been recorded, and this number is continuously increasing. The area has yet to be fully developed, and new exploration is still taking place.

Ratings herein are consistent with those found in the *Mount Woodson Bouldering* guide by Professor Keith A. Brueckner. This inexpensive little book is generally available in San Diego climbing shops, and it is highly recommended. It is a concise and complete introduction to MOUNT WOODSON's more popular climbs. Brueckner updates the work regularly, and thus the most current new routes can be found there.

DIRECTIONS

Take the Escondido-San Diego Freeway (15) to its intersection with Poway Road. Take Poway Road east, through the town of Poway, to a "T" (signal controlled) intersection with Highway 67. Turn left (north) and look for Mount Woodson Road, which appears on the left in 2.7 miles. Continue on Highway 67 a short distance past Mount Woodson Road to a side road on the right (just beyond a sign marking a fire station). Park on this side road, and take trail from the fire station gate to the paved road that leads up MOUNT WOODSON. The first boulders are encountered a couple hundred yards up this paved road.

Alternatively, it is possible to reach Woodson from the east side of San Diego by picking up Highway 67 from Interstate 8.

POISON OAK

There's quite a bit of poison oak in and around some of the popular bouldering sites, and climbers should be alert to its possible presence.

DIRECTION FINDING

The text which follows includes climbing information for twenty boulders. These have been labeled A - T for easy cross-reference with the accompanying map (the A - T designations are for convenience only; they are not official boulder names).

All directions for left or right of road are given from the perspective of a person walking uphill. Also, compass references are typically used — both in terms of locating boulders and in finding routes on a given boulder. These are only approximations, and a quick glance at the accompanying map should be sufficient to orient oneself.

BOULDER A

Boulders A & B are easily identified as they are the first two boulders encountered along the paved access road. Boulder A is on the left side.

1.	**Crack**	**5.10D (5.10A)**

Ascend the thin crack on the east face (visible from road). This is 5.10D if climbed directly; 5.10A if face holds are used.

2.	**Flake**	**5.6**

Ascend flake on west (uphill) side of boulder.

BOULDER B

Boulder B is located on the right-hand side of the road, directly opposite Boulder A. The flake on the south side (facing road) is 5.8.

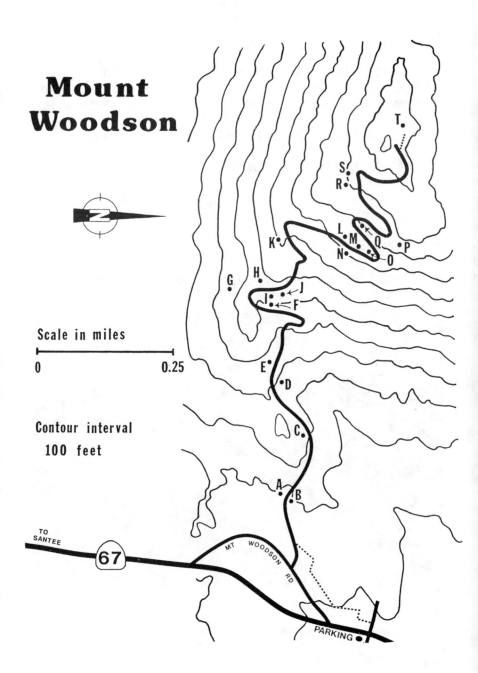

Mount Woodson

Scale in miles

0   0.25

Contour interval 100 feet

TO SANTEE

67

MT WOODSON RD

PARKING

BOULDER C

This boulder is located about 80 yards up the road from the previously mentioned Boulders A & B. Hike past a gate, and continue about 50 yards uphill. At this point, look for a large boulder about 50 feet above the road on the left. There are two classic routes on the side which faces the road. These are:

1. **I HEAR MY TRAIN A' COMIN'**   5.11C

    Climb the long overhanging crack which ends in a dihedral. Can be top-roped.

2. **RAZOR'S EDGE**   5.10D

    Lieback up the thin flake on boulder's northwest corner (to right of Route #1 above).

Overview of Mt. Woodson, showing locations of three popular bouldering sites: Boulder E (SECOND TOWER), Boulder H (UNCERTAINTY PRINCIPLE), and Boulder F (ROBBIN'S CRACK).

BOULDER D   (ELEPHANT'S TRUNK)

Continue hiking up the road till a rounded boulder is visible on the right, about 50 feet below the level of the road. This boulder has an overhanging crack on its east face (visible from road). The crack is 5.9.

BOULDER E   (SECOND TOWER —
see accompanying photo)

SECOND TOWER is the large isolated boulder on the left hillside. It's easily identified by the obvious chimney on its north corner.

1.   Chimney   5.8

Climb the obvious chimney formed by a split in the rock. It's on the right-hand downhill corner of the tower.

2.   Offwidth   5.7

This is the crack on the uphill side of the split which forms Route #1 above.

3.   Face   5.9

The route goes up the center of the face to the right of Route #2. Commonly done as a top-rope problem. To establish a top-rope belay, ascend Route #2 to reach rappel/belay bolts on top of boulder.

BOULDER F (See accompanying photo)

Boulder F is located on the right hillside about 120 yards past the point where the road takes its first sharp switchback turn. There are three classic routes on this boulder:

1. LIE DETECTOR 5.12

This is the obvious crack on the east side of the boulder (facing road).

2. ROBBIN'S CRACK 5.10A

Ascend the hand crack on the uphill side of the boulder.

3. ERIC'S PROBLEM 5.11B

Climb corner to the left of ROBBIN'S CRACK, then transfer to face on left about half-way up. Commonly done as a top-rope problem — ascend ROBBIN'S CRACK to utilize belay/rappel bolts on top.

Rudy DeLeon on Robbin's Crack.

BOULDER G (SICKLE CRACK)

Leave the paved road at the switchback above ROBBIN'S CRACK (Boulder F), and scramble over to the large fragmented boulder about 75 yards south of the road. SICKLE CRACK (5.8) is the 25 foot high curving crack on this boulder's downhill side. Bolted on top.

BOULDER H (UNCERTAINTY PRINCIPLE)

Just above ROBBIN'S CRACK (Boulder F), the road switchbacks towards the north. After this turn, there is a large and prominent triangular boulder on the left hillside (above the road). UNCERTAINTY PRINCIPLE (5.11D) is on the overhanging east face, which is the face visible from the road.

BOULDER I

About 50 yards beyond UNCERTAINTY PRINCIPLE (Boulder H), there is a large boulder which overhangs the road to the left. Immediately opposite (on the right-hand side) is a boulder with a face downhill and away from the road. This boulder is further identified by being directly uphill from ROBBIN'S CRACK (Boulder F). The downhill face has a short sloping finger-crack (5.6).

BOULDER J (DRIVING SOUTH)

About 50 yards past Boulder I, there is a similarly positioned rock; i.e., on the right-hand side, with face below and away from road. DRIVING SOUTH (5.11C) is the crack which splits this downhill face.

BOULDER K

The paved access road turns to the southeast at the third switchback, and then passes underneath a utility line before reaching the fourth switchback. At this point (underneath the utility lines), take a scrambleway which leads to the left. Boulder K is about thirty yards to the south.

1.   **JAWS**   **5.11A**

The boulder is split through by a crack. JAWS ascends the north side of this crack — starting inside a deep cleft in the rock.

2.   **BABY ROBBINS**   **5.9**

Ascend finger crack on south side of boulder (this is the opposite side of the split which forms JAWS).

BOULDER L

About 50 yards before reaching LUNCH ROCK (see Boulder M), Boulder K is found on the left hillside. It's marked by two left-sloping cracks.

1.   **Undercling**   **5.10A**

Lieback the left-hand crack.

2.   **Face**   **5.10A**

Face climb up shallow dihedral to right of the undercling.

BOULDER M (LUNCH ROCK)

After JAWS (Boulder K), the road switchbacks again — this time angling northeast for a long and relatively straight section. Near the end, there is a long and smooth (almost slab-like) face along the left edge of the road. This is LUNCH ROCK; it's easily identified by the prominent zig-zag chimney directly overhead. There are numerous short face climbs (5.5 - 5.9) on LUNCH ROCK.

BOULDER N

Boulder is on the right-hand side of the road, immediately opposite LUNCH ROCK.

1. **POISON OAK CRACK**   5.7

Ascend the fist crack on the side facing the road. There are two bolts at the top left.

2. **WERNER'S CRACK**   5.11B

This is on the same boulder as POISON OAK CRACK, but it's on the opposite (east) face (that is, the side downhill and away from the road). Route starts with a hand traverse to and around a corner, then continues straight up.

BOULDER O

About 20 yards beyond LUNCH ROCK (Boulder M), there is a long low boulder to the left; it's split approximately in the middle by an overhanging hand/fist crack. This is MONKEY CRACK (5.10C).

BOULDER P

Just past MONKEY CRACK (Boulder O), the road switchbacks to the southwest. From this switchback, Boulder P is clearly visible on the hillside above — it's a large boulder with a crack on the left and a prominent split on the right. ELIZA'S CLIMB (5.5) goes up the left crack.

BOULDER Q (MOTHER SUPERIOR)

Just past the sixth switchback, MOTHER SUPERIOR is found on the right-hand side below the level of the road. It's an overhanging offwidth crack, and it starts from a deep slot between two large boulders. MOTHER SUPERIOR splits near the top — take either branch; the crux is at the bulge below. 5.11C

*Location of Boulder R (BAT FLAKE) and
Boulder S (ALCOA & STAIRWAY TO HEAVEN).*

BOULDER R (See accompanying photo)

Boulder R is visible to the left of the road, about 50 yards below the 8th switchback. BAT FLAKE (5.10D) ascends the large curving detached flake on this boulder's left corner.

BOULDER S (See accompanying photo)

Boulder S is located about 20 yards west of BAT FLAKE (Boulder R). It contains two classic climbs, both of which are currently in vogue. They are both on the overhanging southwest face of the boulder.

1. **ALCOA**   **5.11D**
   Lieback the right-hand edge of the above-mentioned face.

2. **STAIRWAY TO HEAVEN**   **5.12A**
   Ascend center of overhanging southwest face.

BOULDER T

The paved road branches just before reaching the summit of Mount Woodson. Take the right-hand fork, and proceed about 250-300 yards downhill (passing through an area of numerous antennas). Just beyond the antennas, look for a large boulder on the left — it's easily identified by two long overhanging cracks.

1. **TEST TUBE**   **5.11A**
   Ascend left crack.

2. **CRUCIBLE**   **5.10B**
   Ascend right crack.

Mark Tillman climbing Crucible

25

LA JOLLA BEACH

Beach climbing has its obvious good points, especially on a hot summer day. When the heat makes other San Diego sites unbearable, locals head to LA JOLLA. The climbing is not the best, but the atmosphere certainly is. Cool breezes, refreshing temperatures, and the proximity of the ocean makes for an unbeatable combination. Be sure to take along swimming trunks, ice chest, and — if you wish — dinner for the barbecues.

There are two primary climbing sites at LA JOLLA: Boomer Beach and the People's Wall. The former is natural sea cliff, the latter is man-made retaining wall; both are described in more detail below.

BOOMER BEACH

The best sea cliff climbing is at Boomer Beach in Ellen Browning Scripps Park (see map and directions). The climbing area starts just down the coast from La Jolla Cove and extends for most of the length of the park.

The rock can be nasty: It's dirty, gritty, and slippery. And don't expect to find any well-defined routes or holds; there is a conspicuous absence of both. For the most part, climbers are left to their own devices to find and develop bouldering problems. Typically these fall into one of two categories: 1) face climbing on rounded holds to reach mantles above, or 2) traverses. The second offers the best possibilities, and traverses of up to 150 feet in length have been accomplished. The climbing tends to be difficult; you'll be hard pressed to find a decent mantle or respectable traverse of less than 5.9 ratings.

PEOPLE'S WALL

People's Wall is located at the intersection of Coast Boulevard and South Coast Boulevard, about one-half mile down from Boomer Beach. It's formed of cut rock placed with the flat sides out, and

(continued on page 188)

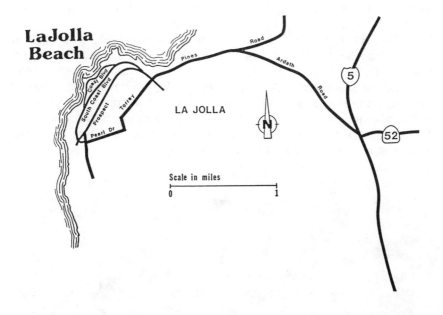

DIRECTIONS

Exit Interstate 5 on Ardath Road, and head west towards Torrey Pines Road. Turn left onto Torrey Pines, then right on Prospect. Once on Prospect, turn right onto either Cave Street or Girard Avenue to reach Boomer's Beach in Ellen Browning Scripps Park. The People's Wall is about one-half mile to the south of Scripps Park.

it abounds with great holds. The primary attraction is a traverse which runs about 70 yards across the middle section of the wall. Handholds are, on the average, about halfway up the 20 - 25 foot high wall. Sections of the traverse are quite easy; however, the full traverse is about 5.9 in difficulty. This is a classic workout site, and the People's Wall is highly recommended.

Also of note in the vicinity of People's Wall is a classic climbing problem on the sea cliff below. This is the "Cave" (see photo); it's located on the beach immediately below the lefthand edge of People's Wall. As seen facing into the cave, climb the left outside corner to reach better holds across the top. This route is quite difficult, but enjoyable (and rather photogenic too). Though the landing is typically soft, it might be wise to have a couple friends along to serve as spotters.

Climbing activity on the People's Wall

Chris Hsu bouldering at the "Cave," La Jolla Beach

26

MISSION GORGE

Overview of Mission Gorge, with the following landmarks shown:

A.	Nob Job	B.	Nutcracker
C.	Trapeze	D.	Lunch Rock

MISSION GORGE is a rather special San Diego site, unique in that it features crag climbing rather than bouldering. "The Gorge" (as it's known locally) is a steep bluff of metamorphic rock broken by numerous cracks and buttresses. The climbing is generally good, though the rock tends to be gritty, and one's first impression is often not overly favorable. There are, however, some truly classic routes which justify putting up with all the unpleasantries, which—in addition to the above-mentioned grittiness—includes the drive, the heat, and the occasional rattlesnake.

There have been five guidebooks to MISSION GORGE. Of all these, the only one that is generally available is *A Photo Guide to Climbs in Mission Gorge* by David Gerberding. This booklet lists 87 climbs, 20 of which are presented in the following pages. Most can be either top-roped or lead; bring gear appropriate to your preference.

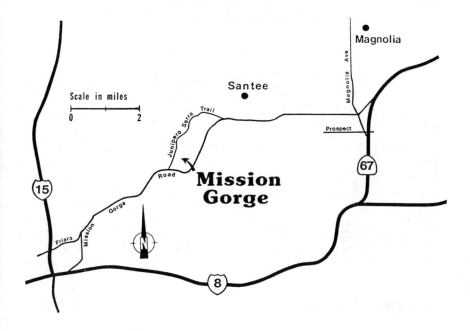

DIRECTIONS

From the 15 Freeway, exit onto Friars Road and head east. In approximately 1¼ miles, Friars Road merges with Mission Gorge Road (alternatively, Mission Gorge Road can be reached directly from Interstate 8). Continue on Mission Gorge Road to Father Junipero Serra Trail, which is 3¼ miles east of the Friars Road/Mission Gorge Road intersection. Turn left onto Father Serra Trail (this turn is easily identified by a large sign marked "Mission Trails Regional Park").

Once turning onto Father Junipero Serra Trail, look for small turnouts on the right about 6/10ths mile up the road. Park here; the climbing sites are above you on the hillside to your right. From the parking area, a 10 minute hike up a "trail" leads to the base of the bluff.

"The Gorge" is located in Mission Trails Regional Park. The road through the park is closed from sunset to sunrise, so plan your visit accordingly.

MAIN CLIMBING WALL, LEFT

1. **NOB JOB**   5.8

    There's a short face with a prominent knob at the extreme northern edge of the main wall. Climb to knob from right, then mantle up and over.

2. **CHIMNEY**   5.2   (Not visible in photo)

    Ascend obvious large chimney to the right of route #1.

3. **ROCK ON**   5.10+   (Not visible in photo)

    Ascend the smooth face just right of the Chimney (route #2). Start in the outside corner and climb to the bolt above.

4. **HANGMAN'S CLIMB**   5.9

    This route angles up and right, following a pair of thin parallel cracks.

5. **OBVERSE FROM THE GAP**   5.11

    This route angles up and left, starting in the broken corner to the right of Hangman's Climb (route #4). The crux is the beginning.

MAIN CLIMBING WALL, LEFT

193

6. OWL   **5.6**

Ascend the off-width crack at left edge of main orange-tinted
face. The climb starts from a wide ledge, which is about 15
feet above the ground.

7. MISSION IMPOSSIBLE   5.11+

This climb starts from the ledge mentioned in route #6. Follow
a hairline crack as it curves up and right. Very strenuous and
awkward, but a true classic.

8. NUTCRACKER   5.9

Ascend the ramp to the right of the ledge (described in Route #6) to reach a shallow recession with cracks in both the left and right-hand corners. NUTCRACKER follows the left crack.

9. GALLWAS CRACK   5.9

Ascend the right crack described in route #8 above.

10. WASP 5.11

Ascend the long & thin crack in a shallow corner, using old pin scars for fingerholds.

11. LILLEY'S DELIGHT 5.7

Climb the corner just left of the roof of GENERAL DYNAMICS (see route #12).

12. GENERAL DYNAMICS 5.10+

Climb up to and over the roof just left of the more prominent overhang of TRAPEZE (see route #14). Requires an awkward heel lock over one's head.

13. EXIT STAGE LEFT 5.9

Ascend the dihedral of TRAPEZE, but bypass the crux by exiting to the left.

14. TRAPEZE 5.11

Ascend the dihedral, exiting via a strenuous finger crack to the right. Requires an over-the-head heel lock similar to that of GENERAL DYNAMICS.

MAIN CLIMBING WALL, RIGHT CENTER

MAIN CLIMBING WALL, RIGHT

(LUNCH ROCK AREA)

15. THE STAIRS   5.3

Follow broken steps up the prow which is immediately above the lefthand corner of Lunch Rock.

16. THE RAMP   5.7

Follow obvious crack system to the right of route #15 above.

17. LUNCH ROCK JAMCRACK   5.8

Ascend the classic jamcrack on the outside face of Lunch Rock (the large flat-topped boulder near the center of the accompanying photo).

18. SKYLINE CHIMNEY   5.4

Ascend the obvious left-leaning chimney above Lunch Rock.

19. BEAUTIFUL   5.4

Ascend the obvious left-leaning crack to the left of SKYLINE ARETE (route #20).

20. SKYLINE ARETE   5.6

Start in the notched corner, follow a large flake up and left, and continue to the bolts above.

MAIN CLIMBING WALL, RIGHT
(Lunch Rock Area)

27

SANTEE

The SANTEE bouldering area is a small boulder-strewn valley located just east of San Diego proper. The site has much to recommend it. The boulders are solid granite, and they have hundreds of classic problems. SANTEE is known primarily for its face climbing, which is superb. There are also numerous mantles, most of which are quite difficult. Finally, there are a few cracks. Though limited in number, the cracks are nonetheless of high quality.

All this diversity makes SANTEE an ideal site for climbers of every experience level. Some of the routes are so easy that they are suitable for the complete beginner. On the other extreme, faces can be found which are so thin that they intimidate even the most advanced boulderer. Top-roping is occasionally recommended (especially for beginners); however, the majority of the routes are short and do not require a rope.

SANTEE is suitable for climbing year round, but summer days can get quite hot. At that time of year, the climbing is best in early morning or late afternoon/evening.

Easy access has made SANTEE more popular than one would normally expect for an area so limited in size. It's possible to take a dirt road very close to the boulders. However, a note of caution is in order; it's illegal to park off the paved road, and you risk getting a ticket if you use the dirt road. On the other hand, if you choose to park on the pavement, keep in mind that the area is residential. To maintain good relations with the inhabitants, boisterous behavior would best be avoided.

Caution: rattlesnakes are occasionally encountered.

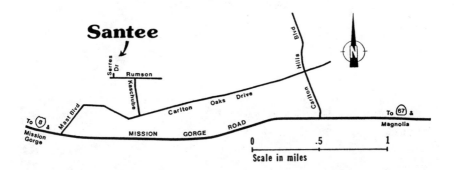

DIRECTIONS

SANTEE is located a few miles east of MISSION GORGE; consult that map for an overview of the general area and for directions to Mission Gorge Boulevard. In the town of Santee, turn north onto Carlton Hills from Mission Gorge Boulevard. Turn left on Carlton Oaks and proceed for a couple miles to Kaschube. Turn right on Kaschube, then left on Rumson, then right again onto Serres. Either park here or take the dirt road into the climbing area.

Alternatively, Carlton Oaks may be reached from Mast Boulevard (see map above).

OVERVIEW OF SANTEE, WITH ARROWS SHOWING LOCATIONS OF BOULDERS DESCRIBED IN TEXT.

A.   BIG HUNK

B.   DOG PILE

C.   SUZY'S MANTLE

D.   BLACK DOT

E.   CAROUSEL (Not visible in photo — located behind "Black Dot)

F.   NORTH MUDBALL

G.   SOUTH MUDBALL

H.   BEEHIVE WALL (Not visible in photo — located behind "Moby Dick")

I.   MOBY DICK

J.   BULLET HOLE WALL (Not visible in photo — located behind "Amphitheatre")

K.   THE AMPHITHEATRE

L.   OW ROCK

M.   PAINTCRACK ROCK

N.   DONKEY DICK

For the sake of easy reference, compass points of direction are given. These are approximate only, and correspond to the general north-south trend of the valley. As you approach the climbing sites, the boulders to your left are on the west hill, and those to the right are on the east hill. Boulders are described in the order shown on the accompanying photograph, which is not necessarily the best order for visiting them. If you are new to Santee, you would probably most enjoy the boulders on the east hill, specifically The Amphitheatre and Bullet Hole Wall.

A. BIG HUNK

"Big Hunk" is the large solitary boulder which lies on the north edge of the west hillside. Its sloping north face is ideal for the practice of balance and friction. This face can be climbed almost anywhere, and all of the routes are comparatively easy. "Big Hunk" thus appeals primarily to beginners.

B. DOG PILE

"Dog Pile" is the large grouping of boulders that is the dominant feature of the western hillside. More than twenty routes have been identified on it, primarily on the downhill boulder of the grouping.

The following routes are on the eastern boulder of the "Dog Pile"; that is, the rock to the downhill side of the large central block.

1. Lieback   5.6

Lieback the right-leaning crack on the left edge of the downhill face.

2. Face   5.9

Ascend the sloping face a few feet to the right of route #1.

3.   **Face (various)**   **5.8 to 5.10**

Several climbs can be found on the right edge of the downhill face and around the corner to the right.

4.   **Crack (two)**   **5.6**

On the northeast corner (of the downhill boulder) there are two cracks which converge to form a large triangle on the rock. The left crack is larger; the right is quite thin. Both are 5.6.

The following routes are on the western boulder of the "Dog Pile"; that is, the rock to the uphill side of the large central block.

1.   **Crack**   **5.8**

This is the short crack on the left edge of the south face.

2.   **Face (various)**   **5.9 to 5.11**

Several face climbs can be found to the right of route #1.

3.   **Face**   **5.8**

Ascend the face just right of the southeast corner (of the western boulder). This route lies close to the large central block.

C.   **SUZY'S MANTLE**

"Suzy's Mantle" is the lowest of the large boulders on the western hillside, and it lies immediately downhill from the dominant "Dog Pile." "Suzy's Mantle" is further identified by the sloping slab-like appearance of its east (downhill) face. The following problems are recommended:

1. **Suzy's Mantle**   5.10

   A smaller rock abuts the downhill side of this boulder.
   Mantle onto the obvious hold about six feet to the right
   of this smaller rock.

2. **Mantle**   5.8

   Mantle onto the obvious hold which is about two feet to
   the left of the smaller rock referred to in route #1.

3. **Face**   5.5

   This route is on the northwest corner of the boulder and
   is identified by the cup-shaped flake imbedded in the
   ground. Step off the flake and ascend the corner above.

4. **Flake**   5.5

   Face climb to a flake, which is about five feet to the left
   of route #3. Follow flake to top.

D. **BLACK DOT BOULDER**

   "Black Dot" is the first of two smaller boulders which lie
to the northwest of Santee's little central valley. ("Black Dot"
is about 50 yards northeast of "Suzy's Mantle"). A classic 5.10
face climb goes up the northeast face, just left of an obvious
split in the rock. Climb up to the "black dot" itself, a tiny
round and thin black foot-hold. Easier face climbs (about 5.8
to 5.9) can be found around the corner to the left.

E. **CAROUSEL**

   "Carousel" is the second of the two smaller boulders
which lie to the northwest of the central valley. ("Carousel" is
about 20 yards northeast of "Black Dot"). Despite this
boulder's small size, there's quite a variety of excellent climbs
here. Carousel can be climbed almost everywhere, and a
traverse (5.10) goes around the entire rock.

The following three climbs are on the north face:

1. **North face, left**   5.9

   Step off flake and climb to pocket up and right.

2. **North face, center**   5.9

   Start on a good foot-hold (beneath the low undercling) and head straight up the rock.

3. **North face, right**   5.8

   Climb up the thin flakes immediately to the right of route #2.

F.   NORTH MUDBALL

   The "Mudballs" are the two northernmost boulders on the east hillside. The left one is easily identified by its three prominent cracks and is known locally as the "North Mudball."

   The following routes are recommended:

1. **Left Crack**   5.4

   Actually this is a unique combination of two cracks and a shallow chimney. Climb using either jamming or chimney technique (or a combination of both).

2. **Center Crack**   5.5

3. **Right Crack**   5.1

4. **Mantle**   5.7

   Mantle onto the obvious knob on the corner to the right of the cracks.

G. SOUTH MUDBALL

"South Mudball" is the rock immediately to the right of the easily-identified "North Mudball." This rock is also known as "Lieback Boulder" for reasons which will be obvious once the following routes are attempted:

1. **Crack**   **5.6**

Lieback the finger crack on the left of the main face.

2. **Mantle**   **5.8**

Mantle onto the 2 inch wide angular shelf to the right of route #1.

3. **Corner**   **5.8**

Follow thin crack up southwest corner (to right of route #2).

4. **Face**   **5.8**

Climb to angular shelf, which is five feet to the right of route #3.

5. **Lieback**   **5.10**

Lieback the angular corner four feet to the right of the shelf of route #4.

H. BEEHIVE WALL

The "Beehive Wall" is actually a collection of three boulders located about 20 yards northeast of the landmark "Moby Dick." The two left boulders touch each other, and the right is separated from the formation by about ten feet.

LEFT BEEHIVE

1. **Crack**   **5.9**

Ascend the vertical jamcrack on the left.

2. **Face**   **5.8**

Climb straight up the obvious knobs, about five feet to the right of route #1.

3. **Lieback**   **5.9**

Lieback the right edge of the pillar to the right of route #2.

MIDDLE BEEHIVE

A variety of face climbs can be done on the steep southwest face. Bolted at top for protection; difficulty of 5.10 to 5.11.

RIGHT BEEHIVE

1. **Face (various)**   **5.5 and up**

A variety of climbs can be found on the south face.

2. **Undercling**   **5.8**

Undercling the obvious flake on the southwest corner.

I.   MOBY DICK

"Moby Dick" is the tallest rock at Santee, and it's included here primarily for its value as a landmark. It's located near the center of the eastern hillside; and its height makes it unmistakable. There are some bouldering problems along the base; otherwise there are only two established routes:

1.   **Southeast Corner**   **5.8**

At the corner, follow the bolts to the top.

2.   **South Face**   **5.11**

Head straight up the face left of route #1. Bolted at top for protection.

J.   **BULLET HOLE WALL**

"Bullet Hole Wall" is actually two boulders, with a two foot gap between. They are located immediately west of Moby Dick. Most of the routes are on "Bullet Hole" proper, which is the easternmost of the two boulders.

The following routes are recommended:

1.   **Face (various)**   **5.8 and up**

Several face climbs are on the eastern side of the main boulder.

2.   **Bullet Hole**   **5.10**

Mantle over the top, using the obvious bullet hole which is on the left center of the main face.

3.   **Left Crack**   **5.9**

There are two cracks on the right side of the main wall. the left is thin and hard.

4.   **Right Crack**   **5.7**

Larger and easier than left crack.

5.   **Face (various)**   **5.8 and up**

Variety of face climbs possible on the northwest side of the western boulder. Bolted at top for protection.

K.   THE AMPHITHEATRE

"The Amphitheatre" is located about 10 yards southwest of "Moby Dick." This boulder is probably the most popular climbing site in all of Santee, and it is known for it's classic edging problems. The curving south wall can be climbed virtually everywhere, with routes ranging from 5.6 to 5.10. The same is true for the northeast side (facing "Moby Dick") where a large variety of routes are possible; again 5.6 to 5.10. The routes on the north side (facing "Bullet Hole Wall") are harder, generally 5.10ish.

L.   OW (OFF-WIDTH) ROCK

"OW Rock" is the boulder grouping very near the summit of the eastern hill. It's located about 30 yards west of the prominent and solitary eucalyptus tree.

The following two routes are recommended:

1.   **Off-Width Crack**   **5.10**

Climb the obvious flared crack on the south side.

2.   **Traverse**   **5.9**

Traverse to the off-width crack from the right by using undercling holds in the horizontal crack above.

M.   PAINTCRACK ROCK

"Paintcrack Rock" is the large boulder about 30 yards southeast of "OW Rock." Its dominant feature is the obvious paint-filled crack on the south side. This goes 5.8. There is bouldering on the face to the right, and there are a couple of difficult and exposed face climbs around the corner to the left (5.10 and up).

N.   DONKEY DICK

"Donkey Dick" is the 20-foot high solitary pinnacle located about 50 yards south of "OW Rock." There are no easy routes here, and the climbing is exposed. But if you must, the most common route goes up the right side of the south face (5.10).

Matt Oliphant on the Amphitheatre
(Moby Dick in Background)

28

MAGNOLIA

MAGNOLIA is comprised of three interconnected and boulder-strewn hills located a couple miles east of Santee. MAGNOLIA covers an area much more extensive in size than Santee, and there is much greater bouldering potential. However, it does not have the same easy access (a 15 minute uphill hike is required to reach the better boulders). As a result, MAGNOLIA is much less popular than Santee and is accordingly given less attention herein.

Routes on only six boulders are described in the following pages. They are, however, six of the more popular rocks, and they serve as a good introduction to the site. A rope is recommended for some of the climbs described (the boulders are generally bolted at top). Also, anyone visiting MAGNOLIA should keep in mind that rattlesnakes may be present during the warmer months.

Both MAGNOLIA and Santee are covered in depth by a guidebook, namely the *Climber's Guide to Santee Boulders* by Greg Schaffer and Ted Walker. Unfortunately, this book is not generally available. The San Diego A-16 outlet has a copy which can be read at the store, but not removed. You might wish to consult it for further details — on both MAGNOLIA and Santee.

Schaffer and Walker divide MAGNOLIA into three sites: North Hill, Main Hill, and South Hill. The area covered here is the very summit of the Main Hill. To reach this site, park along the dirt field below the Wesleyan Church (see map & directions). Hike up the steep dirt road to the east, and stay on it as it swings north and turns into a smaller footpath. Continue up a boulder-strewn knoll to reach another dirt road at the summit plateau. Follow this as it winds east to the main summit area.

The summit boulders are recommended primarily because there is a concentration of good routes in a comparatively small area. Boulders are described in the order shown in the accompanying photograph. This photo was taken from the east, thus Boulder A is southernmost of the summit group.

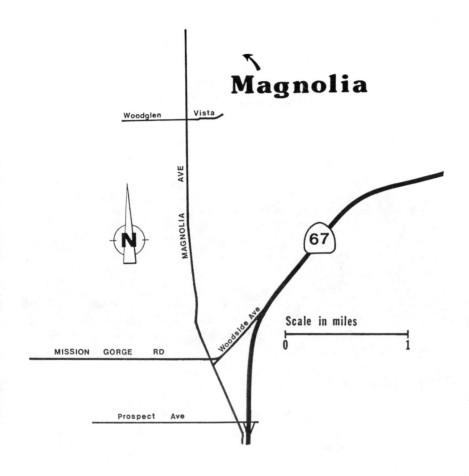

DIRECTIONS

Exit the 67 Freeway at either Prospect or Woodside Avenues (about two miles north of Route 67's intersection with Interstate 8). Make a right-hand turn onto Magnolia Avenue, and proceed north approximately 2½ miles. Park along the dirt field immediately to the south of the landmark Wesleyan Church. See text for walking directions to climbing sites.

NOTE: Magnolia is located a few miles east of Mission Gorge. For an overview of the entire area, refer to the Mission Gorge Map.

OVERVIEW OF MAIN HILL SUMMIT,
MAGNOLIA BOULDERS

BOULDER A

This is the first in a row of four climbable boulders. It's separated from the second by a three foot gap. There are two good face routes here, and they can be protected by top-rope (there's a bolt on top).

1.   SOUTH FACE   5.8

Climb up thin flakes and mantle over the top.

2.   EAST FACE   5.11

The east face has a prominent crack which runs from upper left to lower right.   Start in the crack, then transfer to face as crack narrows.

BOULDER B

This is the boulder that is separated from the preceeding one by a three foot gap. Its northeast side has several good low-angle face routes. These range from 5.9 on the far left to 5.6 on the right. One of the best routes is up the center — step off the flake and head straight up (5.8). Bolted on top.

BOULDER C

This is the third boulder in the row of four. It's easily identified by the north-south running crack that completely splits the rock. There are three good crack climbs, all suitable for beginners:

1. **NORTH CRACK**   5.6

Climb the north end of the deep north-south crack.

2. **SOUTH CRACK**   5.5

The south end of the north-south crack is climbable; however, it's shorter and less enjoyable than the north end.

3. **EAST CRACK**   5.3

Another short and easy climb is the crack on the left edge of the east face.

BOULDER D

This is the northernmost boulder of the row of four. Actually, it's the first boulder that is encountered — assuming that one approaches along the summit road. There are two good routes for beginners:

1. **EAST FACE**   5.3

This route is identified by the orange tint of the face and the jumble of rocks at the bottom. Climb straight up the face using obvious holds.

2.   NORTH CRACK   5.5

Ascend the long low-angle crack located around the corner to
the right of route #1.

BOULDER E
This is the large solitary rock located to the east of the
above-described row of four.   There are several good routes;
however, there is no easy access to the bolt on top, nor is there an
easy descent. This boulder is thus not recommended for beginners.
The better routes are:

1.   EAST FACE   5.10+

Ascend the obvious crack up the center of the steep east face.

2.   NORTHEAST CORNER   5.10

Stand atop a small pedestal and climb straight up the corner.
Very thin.

3.   NORTH FACE (various)   5.9

Several face climbs can be found to the right of route #2.   All
are about 5.9.

4.   NORTHWEST CORNER   5.6

Ascend the short face route on the right edge of the north
side.   Continue up sloping northwest corner to reach the
summit. This is the normal descent route.

5.   WEST FACE   5.8

Ascend the thin crack in the obvious open book, using holds on
the adjoining faces.

BOULDER F (Not visible in photo)

This boulder is located about 25 feet west of the easily-
identified Boulder E (see above).   It's primary attraction is the
obvious lieback up the flake on its south side (5.7).

With all that evolving spread out behind us

We dance this frost fall morning away

On the sunward sides

Of granite boulders

—— Doug Robinson

REFERENCES

The following were consulted in the course of compiling the route information included in the *Climber's Guide to Southern California*. Asterisks (*) denote those works which are mimeographed, photo-copied, underground, out-of-print, or otherwise generally unavailable. The others can typically be found at climbing shops, and they are recommended for anyone desiring to further explore Southern California climbing opportunities.

Bouclin, Robert, Kovach, Dan & Kovach, Steven. *Devil's Punchbowl Climber's Guide.* Lancaster, 1976. (*)

Brueckner, Keith A. *Mt. Woodson Bouldering.* La Jolla, 1986.

Cobb, G. *A Guide to Big Rock Climbing.* Perris, CA (*)

Fry, Craig. *Southern California Bouldering Guide.* Evergreen, CO: Chokstone Press, 1990.

Gerberding, David. *A Photo Guide to Climbs in Mission Gorge.* San Diego: Ilynx Books, 1983.

Harlin, John III. *The Climber's Guide to North America, V.I: West Coast rock Climbs.* Denver: Chockstone Press, 1984.

Hellweg, Paul & Fisher, Donald B. *Stoney Point Guide.* Glendale: La Siesta Press, 1982.

Katz, David. *Getting High in L.A.,* 1990.

Mackay, Steve. *A Climber's Guide to Mt. Rubidoux,* 1984. (*)

Mayr, Troy. *Sport Crags in Southern California.* Evergreen, CO: Chockstone Press, 1992.

Schaffer, Greg & Walker, Ted. *Climber's Guide to Santee Boulders.*
San Diego, 1982. (*)

Tucker, Stephen. *Climbing in Santa Barbara and Ventura Counties.*
Santa Barbara, 1981.

Vogel, Randy. *Hunk guide to Orange County.* Santa Ana: Bonehead
Publishing, 1982.

Vogel, Randy. *Rock Climbs of Tahquitz and Suicide Rocks.* Denver:
Chockstone Press, 1985.

Vogel, Randy. *Joshua Tree Rock Climbing Guide.* Denver:
Chockstone Press, 1986.

White, Doug, ed. *Crags & Boulders of San Diego County.* San Diego:
1978. (*)

Wilts, Chuck, ed. *Tahquitz and Suicide Rocks.* New York: The
American Alpine Club, 1979.

Wolfe, John & Dominick, Bob. *A Climber's Guide to Joshua Tree
National Monument.* Diamond Bar: Desert Rats
Uninhibited , 1976.

ABOUT THE AUTHORS

PAUL HELLWEG

Paul Hellweg is an Assistant Professor in the Department of Leisure Studies & Recreation at California State University, Northridge, where he teaches classes in mountaineering, backpacking, and related subjects. He is the author or co-author of eight books, including two other climbing guides: the *Stoney Point Guide* and the *Mount Whitney Guide for Hikers and Climbers.*

NATHAN WARSTLER

Nathan Warstler is a custom guitar builder at Yamaha's U.S. research and development facility. He is also a previously published photographer, has practical experience in many of the fine arts and holds a Bachelor of Arts degree. In addition, he has assisted in the teaching of climbing, backpacking and wilderness survival classes at the university level.